Better Boundaries

Owning and Treasuring Your Life

Jan Black & Greg Enns

D0962372

NEW HARBINGER PUBLICATIONS

Publisher's Note

Distributed in Canada by Raincoast Books

Copyright © 1997 by Jan Black and Greg Enns
        New Harbinger Publications, Inc.
        5674 Shattuck Avenue
        Oakland, CA 94609
        www.newharbinger.com

Cover design by Poulson/Gluck Design
Edited by Catharine Sutker
Text design by Tracy Carlson

Library of Congress Catalog Card Number: 97-75478

ISBN-13: 978-1-57224-107-7
ISBN-10: 1-57224-107-1

21 20 19
25 24 23 22 21 20

To Lou Black, my true love, friend, and teacher.

—J. B.

To my beloved wife, Sally, with whom I've practiced this
boundaries work, and my children Corban and Hannah.

—G. E.

Contents

Acknowledgments vii

Introduction 1

Part I: Boundaries 7

1 Understanding Boundaries 9

2 How Boundaries Are Formed 23

3 Your Personal Boundary System 29

4 The Guarantees and Challenges 45
  of Boundaries

Part II: Treasuring Yourself 53

5 Becoming Your Own Best Friend 55

6 Knowing What You Think about Yourself 63

7 Understanding the Source and Strength 73
  of Your Self-Beliefs

8 Identifying False Beliefs 97

9 Adjusting the Way You Think 111

10 Getting to Know and Like Yourself 137

11   Embracing Your Purpose, Mission,   161
              and Abilities

12   Making Good Choices   175

Part III: Better Boundaries   181

13   Taking Boundaries to Life Situations   183

Part IV: The Treasured Life   217

14   Successful Stories   219

              References and Further Reading   225

Acknowledgments

I am deeply grateful for the inspiring and motivating love of my family whose names I list with joy: Lou, Ken, Che'lene, Jody, Greta, Greg, Madeline, Jonathan, Riley, Owen, Gracie, Anne, and Bob. I also want to acknowledge the love and support of friends like Teresa, Kathleen, John, Spike, Craig, Pat, Marilee, Sylvia, Jeanie, Ruth, and the infamous First Friday Group. I am grateful to my clients whose lives and pursuit of growth have inspired me and now others, and to those who contributed specifically to this work through interviews and surveys. Special thanks go to Farrin and Catharine, our wonderful editors, to Kristin and Matt for their belief, and, of course, to my co-author Greg Enns, a man of knowledge and sensitivity. For me, this project has been a living classroom producing invaluable lessons about my own boundary system, and for that, too, I say "thank you."
—Jan

Thanks to all those who contributed to our boundaries research, completed questionnaires, participated in group discussions, and shared their boundary experiences in interviews.

Deep thanks go to Jan, my business partner and friend. She is a person of huge talent and class.
—Greg

Introduction

Boundaries deliver more than we could ever describe in a book. Through them, you will gain a wonderful array of built-in benefits that simplify, beautify, and clarify life and relationships. They set the stage for love, strength, happiness, well-being, and enthusiastic service for the good of self and others. If this sounds like a pitch for boundaries, it is. We have experienced and observed their power to very quickly raise a life to a new level of competence and joy. Simply put, boundaries are a life-enhancing system of "yes's" and "no's." They are the stop signs and borders you install to protect yourself so that it is clear that you own your life, make good choices, and pursue the authentic expression of who you are in the way you live, love, give, and relate.

Through years of helping our clients to thrive, we have come to believe that the path to well-placed boundaries is a natural process that begins with treasuring yourself, then moves to taking steps toward owning your life and protecting it. This is both a logical and loving approach and is the path we chart in this book for you. In it, we offer you the tools you will need to install and maintain your personal boundaries.

Setting successful boundaries involves sorting and choosing who and what to let into your life and who or what to keep out. For example, one of our clients installed a boundary between her and a pattern of false beliefs about herself she had acquired from her family. For twenty years or more, the cycle had sucked the inspiration out of her just as a project was getting off the ground. An attitude of "it doesn't matter anyway" that she learned as a child as a way to avoid disappointment would overtake her joy. She would remain mildly depressed until something would inspire her again and the cycle would continue. Instead of fighting it, she had given in to a life and career that required little of her, resulting in boredom and a betrayal of her true creative self. With the help of coaching, she became aware that she did not treasure herself as the smart, innovative person she truly is. By recognizing this pattern and saying "no" to it, and then supporting her decision with an action plan, she immediately experienced a new love toward herself and a sense of ownership and control of her life and future.

The boundaries she set by choosing to recognize and change old false beliefs about herself will protect her from unnecessary internal and external distress, preserve her for pursuit of a positive life, and present her as someone who knows her worth. Boundaries will do the same for you.

In life and the universe, boundaries are essential. In fact, an absence of boundaries guarantees chaos. It is abnormal, unhealthy, and dangerous to exist without them. You are surrounded by an endless parade of boundaries. From the solar system to mathematics to your own body's temperature, boundaries are embedded everywhere, giving structure, guidance, and definition.

Boundaries in nature. Boundaries are essential to a structured, smooth-running life as well as to a structured, smooth-running universe. They maintain order and keep things identifiable. Oceans go so far and stop. Pigs do not mate with horses. Daisies do not become magnolias. Planets stay in their assigned orbits.

Boundaries in geography. In your mind, fly just above the earth. Look down and you will see boundaries. Rivers have banks, roads have shoulders, cliffs have edges, mountains have valleys, countries have borders, and farms have property lines. Each thing has a beginning and an ending that is defined by its boundaries.

Boundaries in cultures. Cultural boundaries exist within nations, companies, religions, and communities. They are formed around things like language, behavior, customs, rituals, beliefs, attitudes, loyalties, skills, and experiences. For example, in some cultures, eating is only allowed with your right hand. The left hand is considered "sinister." Similarly, some cultures value loud and open expression of grief while others honor a more stoic approach. "When in Rome do as the Romans do" speaks to a long-standing need to acknowledge and adapt to a culture's boundaries.

Boundaries in families. Families are famous for the lines they draw around people and behaviors. They adopt spoken and unspoken rules, limits, and ideologies not easily overturned, even in adulthood. The boundaries a family has can be quickly identified by asking the following questions: Can the children speak their minds respectfully? What does the family do on Saturday mornings? When are beds changed? How is money to be saved and spent? Can you drop in on friends or must you always call ahead? How must you dress if you are going to the store? If, how, and when should feelings be expressed? Your personal boundary system not only integrates boundaries you adopted from your family, but also has grown from other influences and experiences in your life.

Other boundaries. Boundaries are endlessly present. Our office overlooks a freeway full of them. Dividers separate traffic patterns, lanes keep cars within the lines, exits and on-ramps guide traffic on and off the freeway, signs set limits on speeding, horns and gestures warn drivers to stay in their place, and an occasional state policeman can be seen helping a driver rethink a boundary violation. The following are examples of everyday boundaries that are common among the millions of people in the world:

- Limits to what your body can physically tolerate
- Rules regulating your behavior in society
- Building codes
- Musical scales
- Engine requirements
- Sales territories
- Recipes and baking times
- Zip codes
- Noise levels
- Curfews

- End zones
- Budgets
- Deadlines

We repeat, to ourselves and to you, boundaries are essential. This list exemplifies the many ways we live our everyday lives within boundaries. This book, however, will help you create *personal* boundaries. To try to thrive without them will lead to failure.

Most boundaries are flexible; some are inflexible. Some people think of flexible boundaries as fences with gates or wheels. You move them to fit the situation and your own growth. For example, Tom, a client once blocked from satisfying interaction by a compulsive need to talk too much, installed a boundary that restricted him from saying more than five sentences at a time. Once he grew as a listener, he gradually moved the boundary aside and is now able to interact successfully. As you create better boundaries, you will learn which ones can be more flexible to match the circumstance.

However, you may need certain boundaries to be inflexible. You might think of them as fences with no entrances or exits. These kinds of boundaries don't move easily, if at all. Inflexible boundaries are appropriate when you need to protect yourself from something or someone that has proven harmful to you. For example, someone who was once easily swept into controlling relationships may choose to build an inflexible boundary against dating people who show early signs of attempting to dictate his or her behavior. Similarly, people who have defined and chosen certain moral standards will build inflexible boundaries between themselves and what they consider to be immoral behaviors. Both flexible and inflexible boundaries give structure to your life. Your boundaries will define who you are, who you give time and energy to, where you're headed, and what you care about.

Better Boundaries

As we have said, this book will chart a path that takes you from treasuring yourself, to owning your life, to protecting it with well-placed boundaries. Our goals are to increase your knowledge and skills so you can thrive. In part 1, we identify boundaries to help you create better ones. In part 2, we focus on the subject of treasuring yourself because people are more inclined to protect what they value. Part 3 is composed of examples of life situations centered on boundary issues. Finally, in part 4 we conclude with a brief view of clients of ours who are living treasured lives.

The following list of definitions are words we use throughout the book—just familiarize yourself with them to help avoid confusion later.

Boundaries: A limit you set between yourself and people due to thoughts, activities, and things that aren't in your best interest.

Self: Your most authentic physiological, psychological, and spiritual self.

Purpose: Your core motivation and contribution.

Mission: The expression of your purpose.

Treasuring Yourself: Befriending, valuing, and loving yourself as a treasure.

Spirit: Your innermost core of being; your essence.

Writing this book has strengthened our own personal boundary systems and we are sure that reading it can do the same for you.

Part I

Boundaries

1

Understanding Boundaries

"The appropriate uses of the words 'Yes' and 'No' make more room for love."

—SARK

You protect what you care about. If you care about your Self, you will protect yourself with personal boundaries unless you don't know how, or don't know it's your right.

It's impossible for you to thrive without strong boundaries, and the most stable boundaries seem to be rooted in the ability to treasure yourself. When you are clear on where you end and others begin, when you adopt full ownership of your life, and when you're your own best friend, you will naturally build better boundaries and therefore a finer, more caring life. The gain is too great and the loss too devastating to treat this like a non-essential. In very real ways, your life can literally depend on boundaries.

The Essential Need for Boundaries

Researchers in every field of human study agree that boundaries are essential to a meaningful, well-lived life. They promote health, inner peace, safety, confidence, exploration, expression, positive relationships, and service to others. The best way to define boundaries is probably to just say what they do.

Boundaries define your identity. Boundaries are your borderlines, enabling an identifiable shape to emerge around your beliefs and preferences. This definition produces a confidence within you that lets others know what you have to offer. You become like a product with clearly defined ingredients. People can sense that you are clear and confident with yourself. They will know what to expect from you. This doesn't mean boundaries make you predictably boring; it means they help you attract positive people and opportunities that will welcome who you are.

Boundaries protect you from violators. Boundaries protect you from people, beliefs, habits, and situations that lessen or block you in some way. "Violators" are not so attracted to people with good boundaries because it is tougher to manipulate or control someone with clearly defined boundaries. Boundaries are like a sorting machine that says "yes" to what fits and "no" to what doesn't. They let in what is good and keep out what is bad so that you remain safe to be and express your authentic self. Boundaries are your border guards; friendly but firm, welcoming but choosey.

Boundaries speak for you. People with effective boundaries give off an often unspoken message that usually discourages boundary violators. Just as self-defense teachers help students learn to walk a certain way to project an "I'm prepared if you mess with me" attitude, boundaries help your personna "walk" a certain way that says "I'm open but particular." Vandals think twice when they sense this kind of confidence.

Boundaries bring order. The reason you require clear boundaries is that without them you will be unable to regulate the coming and going of swarms of people, demands, ideas, dreams, commitments, responsibilities, opportunities, pleasures, and activities. Without boundaries, life becomes a transit station without a train schedule—chaotic, going this way and that on the whim of an engineer or the threats of passengers. It is internal anarchy resulting in personal warfare and ultimately the death of a vibrant, intentional life.

Boundaries attract respectful relationships. Others who also have an effective personal boundary system will be attracted to you, increasing your probability of positive, respectful relationships. Their attraction stems from their own admiration for a person who has made the effort to create boundaries and also from a belief that their own boundaries will be respected. Those without healthy boundaries may be drawn initially to a person of strength, but they're usually scared away when their efforts to control, put down, or manipulate are resisted.

Boundaries promote you. Just as boundaries can speak for you, they can also promote you to people and opportunities looking for someone with your identity, confidence, and self-care. When you are a person with clearly defined boundaries, you know yourself and your strengths. You want to use them in your life and work. Leaders and employers with good boundaries recognize this. They know if you have boundaries you can be more trusted to state clearly what you can and cannot do, offer workable alternatives, welcome input, work passionately without burnout, and stick to projects and jobs that suit your strength. As an employee with boundaries you will also be better able to withstand the inevitable criticism from others at work. They may often be intimidated or angered by their inability to penetrate your ethic and reduce your production or service to their level of mediocrity.

Boundaries protect you from the control of others. You are president of your life and boundaries will protect you from people who want to impeach you. They will also make it difficult for manipulators to control you because you will recognize a threat to your ownership.

Boundaries preserve your purpose and mission. When you know your purpose and mission, you have even more reason to create better boundaries. Once your purpose and mission are identified, boundaries will preserve you for those relationships and opportunities that fit who you are and what you want to do about it. You will be undistracted by sirens of opportunity that would otherwise tempt you to steer off course.

Boundaries protect your finest personal assets. Your knowledge, body, skills, abilities, purpose, and mission are among your finest personal assets. These assets deserve protection, and boundaries

will both protect and preserve them so you can invest them en-
thusiastically across your life.

Boundaries satisfy your need for self-confirmation. When an artist puts lines on paper, a form is defined, or confirmed. When
you draw lines around your life, you and your personality are
defined. Your boundaries confirm you exist and in what form.
For example, if you are an introvert, you will draw a line between
yourself and pressure from others to be "more social." The boundary confirms your true nature.

Boundaries trim away the inauthentic clutter that can hide
you from being seen, acknowledged, and confirmed. This is one
more reason to take them seriously—because they help you to
be taken more seriously.

The New Need for Boundaries

The need for an effective boundary system is increasing constantly
for a number of reasons.

Fewer societal boundaries. You have fewer cultural, political,
and moral boundaries around you than you did last year. And
last year you had fewer than the year before because there is an
ever-increasing removal of established societal lines between what
is acceptable and unacceptable. The loss of cultural norms and
standards makes it even more imperative for you to set your
own. In an age of relativism, where people decide for themselves
what is right, you have to figure out what is right in your own
eyes. Few cultural traditions are doing it for you. As the lines of
established tradition fade, the need for people to create their own
lines intensifies.

Although it has always been important to create a personal
code of ethics and behavior, the number of issues to be decided
personally were fewer because society made some of the choices.
For example, mainstream lines have been lifted around the following: cloning, integrity expectations of public figures, sex outside marriage, abortion, violence and nudity in the media,
accuracy of school grading systems and national testing, protecting children and teens from pornography, living together before
marriage, homosexuality, expression of faith, truth in reporting,
homeschooling, and too many others to name. Right or wrong,
these issues had fairly clear boundaries around them in most

cultures. Now they don't, and each person must decide where his or her lines will be drawn.

Another example of a shift in cultural boundaries is domestic violence, once protected behind the cultural boundaries of privacy. For years, mainstream society in America either turned its head or possibly even chuckled, when a husband "reminded the little lady who's boss." Now the line of privacy has been lifted, forcing people to take a personal position on the issue of domestic violence and abuse in general.

Growing population. More people means more reasons for boundaries. Population taxes the environment. The pace of life quickens. There's more noise, more congestion, and more competition. More people means more potential relationships. Or more isolation. What will your boundaries be? What will you let in? Keep out? Give? Receive?

Increasing neediness. Neediness among the population in general is also increasing in every aspect of life. Good causes, real crises, and desperate conditions cry out for your help. How will you sort them?

All of these reasons are in addition to the *fundamental* one for setting boundaries: you value and own your life.

What Is a Personal Boundary?

A personal boundary is a line you draw to protect all or a part of your life from being controlled, manipulated, "fixed," misunderstood, abused, discounted, demeaned, diffused, or wrongly judged. Personal boundaries protect your life and preserve your highest potential so that your "ultimate purpose" can be joyfully and effectively fulfilled.

Boundaries keep danger and harm out of your life. Harm can come from people, places, or activities, or it can come from internal beliefs and habits.

Personal boundaries are a set of flexible and inflexible limits that let good in and keep bad out. You get to draw a line around your life because it *is* your life. You are in charge of how you live and develop. You are the guardian of your spirit, mind, and body, the curator of your soul and identity, and the keeper of your dreams. The choice is yours. The rights, privileges, and responsibilities of ownership belong to you because this is Your Life.

Your right to boundaries. Your right to boundaries as owner of your life is not selfish, nor does it violate a faith that trusts a Higher Power for guidance. It is a simple principle of ownership. If you own it, it's yours. You get to make choices for your life. If you treasure your life, you will make choices for its good. If you don't, you won't.

Your quality of ownership. The quality of the choices you make as owner of your life will largely depend on how deeply you treasure yourself.

Treasuring yourself is a skill most children know naturally and many adults have literally or figuratively had beaten out of them. Depending on the parenting style in your home, your early efforts at drawing lines around your life may or may not have been welcomed. For many, line-drawing was dropped because it made the adults uncomfortable. Or, the child wanted to avoid lectures or shaming clucks from relatives and teachers who believed children were willful or disobedient if they expressed an opinion.

However, we don't want to give you the impression that only people with weak boundaries need to adjust them. Some people's boundaries need flexing. They have built walls where only fences are required. They need to "let up."

Constructing a solid, effective personal boundary system takes time. However, once you're successful at setting new limits in one area, it will motivate you to move to the next. "The first boundary I drew was between myself and my habit of saying negative things about myself to others," said Carl, a capable engineer struggling with feeling socially inferior. "Once I got a handle on that, I moved to setting limits on names I called myself, like 'You stupid fool' and 'Loser'." He adds, "I moved from boundary to boundary and gradually my life changed."

Boundaries and Your Personal Mission

Boundaries not only maximize the probability of a happy life, they set the stage for discovering and fulfilling your personal mission. Your personal mission is the way you choose to express your identity, purpose, and passion in your life. To set effective boundaries, you must have a sense of ownership over your life. This same ownership will permit you to make choices for it. Your best life choices will be those that are in line with your personal purpose and mission.

Steve came to us for help in clarifying his purpose and mission in light of an opportunity he faced. He is a bright, social, and animated man in his late thirties. He has never married but has enjoyed long-term relationships, including a current one that may become permanent. Sadly, his mother had died three years before. He loves his immediate family, so after a time living across country, he returned to live with his father. Steve's sisters live nearby and he is very close to their young children.

Steve's parents raised their children to be loving, caring people. However, their underlying message was: "We have taken care of you and someday you will take care of us." Steve came to us torn between his love for his father and family and a chance he had been given to pursue his passion as a violinist in a philharmonic two thousand miles away.

The results of our work with Steve revealed that making music was clearly his purpose, and making music professionally was his mission. The position with the philharmonic suited him well. He had a deep love of city life and culture, but thought of this part of himself as "selfish and unnecessary." Our assessments revealed these cultural appreciations to be an important part of Steve's identity.

Steve felt caught between a desire to pursue his career and a desire to be near his family. He wanted to fulfill his father's wish for his help. This was a challenging boundary and ownership test for him and he wanted to create a solution that would satisfy both sides of himself. He wanted a win-win outcome.

We used a storytelling approach to help Steve find the solution he sought. We wrote a fictional future story as if Steve were describing his life to his nephew twenty years from now. The story told how Steve had said "no" to the philharmonic to live with and care for his father in their midsized town, how it felt to pass up the opportunity, and how he had chosen to express his love of music as a volunteer in a local chamber orchestra in his off time from his job as a music store manager.

The point of the exercise was to help Steve "live through" a choice so that he could change it and choose a story he would rather tell. He returned the following week with his own version. Our story had helped Steve know with some certainty that he would not want to have to describe his life in quite that way. In his own editing of the story he had imagined saying "yes" to the philharmonic's invitation, and he didn't like that ending either. So, as often happens when you seek to be true to yourself, another plan emerged.

Steve decided he would move to a large, culturally rich city (to honor his need for city life and culture) sixty miles away from his father (close enough to check in with his father and be involved with his sisters and their families) and play professionally in a chamber orchestra (fulfilling his purpose and mission). Steve left the door open for changes in the future, and was pleased to have discovered a solution that satisfied his points of tension.

Some would say Steve should have taken the philharmonic position, that there comes a time to leave a parent. Others might say he should stay put. The truth is, it doesn't matter what anyone thinks because it's Steve's life. He weighed his choices as owner of his life and balanced them in a way that was true to what most mattered to him.

Boundaries and Benevolence

Boundaries, purpose, and mission are compatible. So are boundaries and benevolence. In fact, without boundaries, the good things you mean to do can easily get choked out by activities and roles you accept because you think you have to.

Benevolence, or acts of kindness, comes in as many forms as there are expressions of love. The loving words you inscribe in a book, the child you mentor, the fresh bread you take to a neighbor, the newsletters you fold for the American Cancer Society, are all acts of benevolence. Kindness makes a difference, because love makes a difference, and one slice of your love springing from your passion can change a life.

At their best, boundaries built on life ownership and treasuredness will free you to wildly fulfill your mission by contributing to the good of others. It also happens to be one of the finest gifts you can give to yourself.

Building Your Boundaries
on Treasuredness

Recently, the Smithsonian went on the road to treat America to a sampling of its treasures. When the exhibit came to Portland, a local radio station conducted exit interviews, asking guests "What did you enjoy the most?" The overwhelming winner on the day we listened was Dorothy's ruby slippers from *The Wizard of Oz*.

The beloved, magical ruby slippers worn on Dorothy's feet in the classic movie were unofficially voted the most treasured object of the exhibit, even though over time they have become less than ruby. They are treasured.

Imagine that on the final day of the exhibit a drawing was held to give away the slippers. Madeline's name was drawn. She was a true fan of *Oz*, a college junior who had memorized the songs by age three and had watched the video so often she could speak the parts. As a child, she had grown through several sizes of her own shiny red shoes.

Now picture Madeline being escorted to her car by the museum's curator. Hear her ask, "What special instructions do I need to take care of these precious slippers?" His answer is: "Just take care of them in a way that shows you love them and they'll be fine."

What's true for Madeline's ruby slippers is true for you as well. If you treat your life in a way that shows you love it, it will be fine. You will guard it, enjoy it, share it, provide for it, develop it, and display it. You will build a personal boundary system to protect what you treasure.

A Life Without Life-Building Personal Boundaries

By life-building boundaries, we mean limits you set that move you forward in your quest for a full, loving life with meaning. A life without positive, life-building boundaries produces endless problems. A boundariless life goes against the pattern of nature and is therefore destined to become live bait for hungry prey.

The results of an ineffective boundary system are widespread; it affects you and the people you encounter and influence, as well as the work you do. For example, if you are a person with weak boundaries who invites people into the intimacies of your life before you know they are trustworthy, you will not only open the door to victimization, you will put others in your life at risk. This creates an emotional roller coaster for all of you. You will experience a string of confusing and unhappy relationships resulting in distress, self-incrimination, and hopelessness. This will affect all of your other relationships with family, friends, and employers. Your life will be out of control, your attention will be divided, and your work and presence will suffer loss.

On the other hand, if you're a hyperboundaried person who refuses to adjust your opinions when new truth is presented to you, you will remain trapped in your ignorance. This can also have a damaging effect on those around you. Not only can your pride block your growth and cause people to discount you as "close-minded," but those you influence, your kids, spouse, and employees, may be shut off from open interaction with you. They may adopt your walled-off attitude, blocking themselves from growth and truth.

As you can see, consequences reach beyond you to those in your life. What you do leads to what others do in very real ways. Consider the long-range consequences of the following patterns on the people you care about:

- Unkept promises

- Overcommitment of your schedule

- Addictions

- Lies and exaggerations

- Denying health problems

- Perpetual complaining

When you are without life-building boundaries, or when you have walls that keep truth out of your life, you create havoc for you and the people you touch. If you haven't discovered it already, you may hurt yourself and others needlessly. We know. Like everyone else, we have done it ourselves. Poor boundaries hurt.

Loss of respect. Ineffective boundaries usually result in a loss of self-respect and respect from others. In fact, unflattering names are used for boundariless people: spineless, invisible, doormat, easy mark, addict, wishy-washy, slut, sell-out, two-faced, and out-of-control. There are also names reserved for closed-off, walled people: mindless, in denial, bully, controlling, ego-maniac, blind, useless, untouchable, arrogant, anal, and thick-headed.

These names do not fit the treasured life.

Loss of control. If you're living without intentional boundaries, your life is dictated by someone or something else, not your own intentional choice.

We're not suggesting that the boundaried life is without undeniable surprises, or that the well-defined person doesn't experience chaotic periods of life. What we are saying is that the boundaried life will have less distraction, chaos, guilt, irresponsibility, missed opportunities, and spoiled relationships than an unboundaried or hyperboundaried one. Your life will also be more prepared for surprises and catastrophes because you will have less chaos in your life. This will then give you the space and focus necessary to face these circumstances.

People of all backgrounds and family systems have many boundary issues in common. This includes the temptation to either give the control of their lives to others, or be so isolated that helpful relationships and opportunities are kept out. Familiar patterns are hard to give up because it is usually easier to go with what you know than to risk the unknown, even if what is known is hurtful or ineffective.

The downside to this is that you will feel helpless and give up making positive choices for your long-term good. This will lead you to experience a loss of energy and cause you to build your life on minimum daily requirements, which may cause you to compensate through short-term fixes.

Loss of interest. Live long enough without boundaries or with boundaries that keep you imprisoned behind your walls and you will lose interest in life. To some degree, you will give up, become hopeless, and likely experience some degree of depression or anxiety. You may become cynical or act like a martyr. You will become listless and people will find you boring. You will leave a legacy that will become like an orphan because no one will want to adopt it. You will feel like your life is anemic, with just enough energy to stay alive but not enlivened. You will eat, sleep, work, groan, feel used, and fulfill basic responsibilities rather than make choices to live and love fully, to work hard and nobly, to fulfill your purpose, and to contribute passionately to your world.

What Boundaries Are Not

Boundaries are not an excuse to be selfish, irresponsible, arrogant, superior, unwilling to help, judgmental, brutally honest, or rude. Boundaries don't mean you will never bend over backwards to help someone, even when it means you will become overtired doing it. Boundaries do not mean you'll never take a risk and let someone or something into your life you are unsure about. Boundaries don't mean you don't give people a second chance. Boundaries don't mean you will never get "taken" by a clever invader or that your boundaries will be respected by one and all. Boundaries do not mean you will have control over your life completely.

What boundaries do mean is that you exert choice over your life as its owner. You'll choose to bend over backwards to help a friend because you want to be that kind of friend. You'll choose to take risks with people and opportunities because sometimes risks pay off and because you want to be a person who is open to pleasant surprises. You will choose to give certain people a second chance because you know you need second chances, and thirds, and fourths. You will choose to trust a person until they prove they are untrustworthy. You will choose to avoid the idea of "getting your life together" and, instead, you will embrace the idea of getting your life in alignment with your purpose and mission.

Boundaries are a choice. To live without effective boundaries is your choice, but it is not a choice that is in your best interest. Remember, boundaries are in concert with the universe. We hope you'll choose to play well in the band.

Reminding Yourself

- Boundaries are required for a full and meaningful life.

- The most stable boundaries are rooted in a sense of personal treasuredness.

- Boundaries bring order; define your identity; speak for you; attract respectful relationships; promote you; protect you from the control of hurtful people, behaviors, and situations; preserve your purpose and mission; protect your finest personal assets; and satisfy your need for self-confirmation.

- As the world changes, new imperatives for boundaries are being constantly created.

- If you treat your life in a way that shows you love it, you will naturally create a personal boundary system.

- A boundary is a line that separates one thing from another.

- Boundaries are a natural part of the universe and are embedded in daily life.

- A *personal* boundary is a line that separates you from other people, places, or things.

- A life without effective boundaries will result in a loss of respect, vitality, and legacy.

- You have a right to create personal boundaries because you are the owner of your life.

- Boundaries are not an excuse for selfishness or poor character.

2

How Boundaries
Are Formed

When you were an infant, you weren't conscious of being a separate creature from all the rest, according to experts. Eventually you found out. You realized you had edges, a stopping point. There was a "you" and there was an "other." Once this key discovery was made, you were on your way to creating your own set of boundaries. You had once also thought you were the center of the universe and then you found out you were not. So what were you? Your task was to find out. You did it by practicing a behavior, watching for a mirrored response, then making a decision to adopt the behavior, try an alternative, or give it up altogether. Somewhere along the way, you formed an opinion about yourself.

Reactions

You became a living, drooling, toddling laboratory, testing your limits, judging reactions, rethinking your hypothesis, and trying again until you got it "right." Reactions were your biggest cue to whether or not your boundary was a "keeper."

Remember, boundaries define you, so as you formed them you were really forming your definition of yourself, or self-view. You concluded:

- Who you were

- What you believed

- What people thought of you

- What your rights were

- Who you could trust

- What might hurt you

- What you did and didn't do well

- What made people laugh with you or at you

- What you needed to do to get attention

- What you had to do to get your needs met

- What role you were to play

- How lovable you were

Because reactions were the basis for your decisions about who you were and what lines you could draw around yourself to stay separate, it's important to point out that the people who reacted to you as a child had their own personalities, self-views, and circumstances. In other words, their reactions weren't always accurate or appropriate, meaning that your conclusions may not be either. This is why it is important that you reevaluate the beliefs you hold that seem to cause difficulties now.

Parenting Styles

The reactions of your parents to your boundary experiments were generally a result of their parenting style. There are four basic parenting styles:

1. *Democratic:* Family members are able to voice boundaries around feelings, beliefs, and concerns, and decide together on solutions. In some forms of democratic parenting, the parent's vote carries more weight, in others the vote is weighted equally between parents and children.

2. *Authoritarian:* Self-expression and discussion are discouraged; boundaries are determined by the governing parent(s).

3. *Permissive:* There tends to be an absence of established boundaries, guidelines, set responsibilities, and limits. For the most part, children determine their own course.

4. *Ambivalent:* Boundaries that are expressed as policies are erratic and unpredictable: loving–not loving, interested–disinterested, strict–permissive, available–not available, trustworthy–not trustworthy. Most experts agree that ambivalent parenting is the most damaging.

As you can imagine, the parenting style in your home had a significant impact on the development of your early boundaries and probably on your existing boundaries. For example, a four-year-old child in a democratic home would be free to decline a request to entertain friends with a song if she did not want to perform. In an authoritarian-style home, where children are discouraged from going against parental desires, saying "no" to the invitation to perform could provoke shaming, guilt, or physical punishment. The first girl would leave the situation believing in her right to have her feelings respected, thus enabling her to create boundaries around her family without guilt. The second girl would leave believing she cannot put a boundary between what she wants and what others want from her.

Review these typical situations of children testing their boundaries. Imagine them taking place within each parenting style. What would the reactions and conclusions probably be in the democratic, authoritarian, permissive, and ambivalent environments?

- Climbing out of bed and playing instead of sleeping

- Rearranging toys in a room

- Choosing an alternative book to the one Dad plans to read

- Mixing food in an unusual way

- Running off when it's time to kiss the relatives

- Saying "I can't talk right now, I'm playing" when mom asks if the child would like to talk to Grandma

Boundary Benchmarks

Under the right circumstances, a child of three has developed the ability to: (1) be emotionally attached to others yet maintain a separate sense of self, (2) say appropriate "no's" to others without fear of loss of love, and (3) receive "no's" from others without withdrawing emotionally. These are the key beliefs in the successful creation of ownership and boundaries, and can be considered a boundary formation benchmark. Many adults have yet to reach it.

Forming boundaries after childhood. Once you formed boundaries at home, you tried them out on people away from home. You learned to adjust them to fit the person and situation. The reactions continued to define you and your opinion of yourself. This means your self-view and self-definition reflected how people reacted to you—or, your interpretation of how they reacted to you.

Adolescent reenactment. In adolescence, you went through a second period of exploration of boundaries, called a "reenactment," but this time the issues were more adult: sexuality, gender identity, and competition. Again, you tested your boundaries by practicing them in front of your parents, peers, and other influencers. You looked into the "mirror" to see their reactions, made the necessary adjustments, and took your conclusions with you into the next stage of your life, fine-tuning as you went along.

Young adult reenactment. The third stage of reenactment probably happened when you left home, possibly to go to college, start a career, or get married. Suddenly you were faced with a level of freedom and responsibilities you may have never known before. This time the issues were things like: personal responsibility, sexual expression, personal codes, and behaviors. This can be an intense and sometimes confusing time of setting boundaries, testing the consequences, trying again, weighing reactions, and gradually forming your adult boundaries.

Adult boundary development. You are still creating and adjusting your boundaries according to reactions, consequences, changing circumstances, and new beliefs.

If your new beliefs include an upgraded sense of your personal treasuredness, your boundaries will improve, and the process will be simplified. For example, Cindy had a weak spot in her boundary system with her friend Angie. If Angie knew Cindy had a free night, Angie would assume Cindy wanted to spend it with her. She would sometimes buy movie tickets on her lunch hour then call Cindy and say "We're going to a movie tonight, okay?" Angie was a pleasant companion, always ready for fun, but tended to be oversensitive to honest feedback.

Cindy wanted to maintain the friendship, but she also wanted to befriend herself by maintaining control of her own life. Cindy thought through her choices:

- Don't say anything and hope things will change.

- Start making excuses to avoid confrontation.

- Make other plans so when Angie calls, I can honestly say "no."

In the past, Cindy would have adopted a blend of all three of these options. As she looked at them now, however, she rejected them because they weren't the best choices for her own good and Angie's. If Cindy was to be her own best friend, she decided she would treat the situation honestly and with respect. Then it would be up to Angie to decide what to do about it. So, Cindy added a fourth option based on treasuring herself:

- Discuss the situation honestly with Angie, reassuring her but not apologizing for my feelings.

Cindy's commitment to being her own best friend required her to draw a new line between old and new behaviors; between honesty and dishonesty, fear and love, manipulation and truth. This is how treasuredness strengthens boundaries and simplifies the process.

Reminding Yourself

- Your early boundaries were formed by the reactions of your primary caregivers.

- Your boundaries defined who you believed you were.

- The parenting style in your home influenced your boundaries and your belief in your right to set them.

- Boundaries will be strengthened and the process simplified as you deepen your sense of personal treasuredness.

3

Your Personal Boundary System

You already have a personal boundary system. You've spent a lifetime building it. But like a smoke alarm, your boundary system can either be connected and ready to protect you; or it can be hanging by its wires, disconnected, and unable to warn you of danger. In this chapter you will learn the essentials of an effective personal boundary system so you can make the choices you need to create better boundaries.

First, remember the three purposes of boundaries:

1. **To protect you**

2. **To preserve you**

3. **To present you**

Interestingly enough, these are the same goals of a museum security system. Museum security must *protect* the treasures, *preserve* them for continued viewing and use, and *present* the treasures in a way that best supports and encases them.

The elements in a museum security system include the following: guards, stanchions, cases, recorders, and signs. Unseen but present are backup systems, computers, nonuniformed guards, and hidden alarms. Plus there are codes, communication devices, and an overall plan with contingencies. Every effort is made to keep the treasure safe. It makes sense to apply the principles of this system to your life so you, the treasure, can safely thrive as well.

System Essentials

To protect, preserve, and present yourself as the treasure you are, you will require a basic set of essentials. Most of the following security measures are already at work to some degree in your life:

- Signage
- Screening devices
- Alarms
- Guards
- Mirrors
- Recorders
- Stanchions (ropes)
- Backup systems
- Enforcement

Now we will look at each essential so you will know how to use it to set and maintain better boundaries for yourself.

Signage

Even before you step into a museum, signs state the limits:

- Hours the museum is open
- Admission requirements
- Location of entrance and exit
- Warnings of surveillance
- Other instructions as needed

When a person enters the museum, it's assumed they have read the signs. If they haven't, they are still responsible for knowing the rules that are posted. However, because museums under-stand people don't always read signs, they rewrite them on brochures, provide information stations, and/or post the data once again inside the doors.

You can follow this principle by posting "signs" around your life. Think of the many signs you wear now. Each one is giving a certain message about you. If you find yourself attracting a certain type of boundary violator, you may want to analyze your signage to be certain it is saying what you really want it to say. Facial expression, for example, is a sign people use to "read" a person. If you are someone with a naturally sweet, almost naive facial expression, you might find service people don't give you the immediate attention you are entitled to as a customer. This is an example of a boundary violator responding to your signage. There are three things you can do about it: (1) nothing, (2) com-plain, or (3) compensate by increasing your assertiveness a few degrees.

Your Signs

Signs you wear might include

- **The way you look:** clothing, hair, accessories, shoes, style, neatness, appropriateness for the occasion, nails, or skin

- **The way you sound:** words, voice, speech patterns, or laugh

- **The way you move:** stride, posture, gestures, or manner-isms

- **The way you seem:** attitude, spirit, social comfort, pro-fessional ease, or topics you discuss

The signs you wear should be the signs you want to display, so you can reduce the number of misunderstandings and potential boundary violations.

Screening Devices

You own an incredible assortment of built-in screening de-vices, otherwise known as senses. When you activate your senses of sight, hearing, touch, smell, and taste to screen out people and situations that could harm or diminish you, you will stay away from many boundary violators.

When you enter a room, your sensors are already on alert. If you pay attention you will get feedback like, "That voice is too loud," "Her body's too close," "This dip tastes funny," "This room is smoky." This information can be helpful in protecting you. The loud voice may be nothing, or it may be a cue that the person is drunk. Someone who's too close may be charming, but it might also be a sign that the woman doesn't care if you're a married man. The food that tastes funny is your sense of taste protecting you from food poisoning, and seeing that the room is smoky is your sight protecting you from potential breathing problems.

If you treasure yourself, you will want to let your senses do their job of screening and you will pay attention to their warnings.

Alarms

Your senses are your external screeners, but you also have an internal set of alarms. They are your intuition, conscience, emotions, and spirit. Like your external senses, these alarms are on and ready to help protect you and be your own best friend.

Intuition. Intuition knows what words can't explain. It is eager to feed you answers and give you certain knowledge to protect you. The intuition alarm sounds when a situation doesn't seem just right, when a person appears safe but something tells you he or she isn't, or when an opportunity seems too good to be true.

Conscience. Conscience is your Jimminy Cricket notifying you that you're about to violate your Self by going against what you know is right. It is particularly important for you to pay attention to this alarm. Forgiving yourself for not listening to it can be very painful.

For most, conscience sounds its alarm when you do things like lie, cheat, steal, intentionally misrepresent, manipulate, and gossip. Your conscience wants to protect you from self-defeating behaviors, so listen to it and simplify your life.

Emotions. Your emotions are your feelings alarm. They protect you by sending feelings that signal potential boundary challenges. The feelings alarm lets you feel fear, for example, when a stranger approaches you on the street, or when you step up to a microphone to speak. Your fear points out what is upsetting to you, as a guard in a museum might point to a suspicious visitor. Once you identify the source of your fear, you can decide what to do to remove or avoid the threat.

Spirit. Your spirit sounds its alarm to tell you when the most treasured part of your Self has been discounted, diminished, and disheartened. It alerts you to situations or circumstances that threaten your beliefs and values, enabling you to prevent yourself from spiritual harm.

Don's spirit notified him his boundaries were about to be violated when a co-worker started speaking in unfair and demeaning ways about a presentation Don had made. Don felt the alarm sound in his stomach and made a choice to pay attention to his alarm. He interrupted the co-worker and said, "You know, I value input but only from people who can give it constructively and respectfully, so I'm going to ask you to stop evaluating my presentation."

Your spirit is the deepest, truest part of you, and deserves your utmost care and attention. Cooperate with its messages to you and you will be treasuring yourself.

Guards

The guards in your personal boundary system are people you admire, respect, and trust, and will give you feedback on your life when you ask. In effect, you are stationing them at points in your life to notice potential violators from within yourself or from outside.

Jenny's guards are her brother, a neighbor, and her Aunt Irene. She selected these people because she feels safe with them, trusts them to want what's best for her, and respects their decisions in life. She has permission to call them when she wants feedback, and has given them permission to notify her if they notice anything of concern in her life or choices.

Who will you select as your guards?

_____

_____

_____

_____

_____

Mirrors

The mirrors positioned at strategic locations in a museum enable staff to see what visitors are doing in hard-to-see areas. Mirrors in your life will do the same. A mirror's function is to reflect; mirrors in your life will reflect truth back to you. This mirroring is especially helpful in determining what people perceive you to be.

For example, if you think you are an engaging conversationalist yet people do not seem involved or responsive when you are talking, your mirror is telling you that what you think and what they think are two different things.

Or, let's say the opposite is true. You believe you are a marginally interesting person yet people's enthusiastic responses reflect that they find you very interesting. In either situation, the mirror has revealed a truth you may not have seen without it.

In both of these cases, you will enhance your life by finding out why people apparently aren't believing about you what you believe about yourself. In the first case, you may see yourself as friendly, transparent, and a "good person." People may, however, see you as overeager and arrogant. In the second case, you may see yourself as "no big deal," yet people may see you as comfortable with yourself, funny, and safe.

So, mirrors will help you identify beliefs you hold that are not being proved by public response. Mirrors are built-in congruence alarms and, if you let them, will keep you true to your highest, treasured self.

Recorders

Video recorders are now a staple of security systems. In your memory you have a built-in set of recorders, both audio and video, that can help you use your experience to be your own best friend. Within your internal archives, you have stored your life experiences. You can learn from your past. Life experiences can alert you to patterns, people, and situations that reappear so you can protect yourself from repeating a negative outcome.

For example, Brice was about to agree to a three-month European hike with his friend Craig. They had been college friends. Brice's recorder alarm went off when Craig told Brice he didn't have the money for airfare and asked if Brice could loan it to him. Brice paid attention to the alarm sounded by his archives and let his recorders replay similar situations Brice had experienced. During the replay, he saw himself loaning money to other people and not getting repaid in a timely manner, if at all. This information led Brice to explore why people often asked him for loans, and why they didn't feel it necessary to pay Brice back when he did loan them money.

Ultimately, Brice did not loan Craig the money. His recording alarm protected him from continuing a defeating pattern and led him to create a future with limits on loans and repayment plans.

Let the recordings in your archives alert you to threats to your treasuredness.

Stanchions

Stanchions, the velvet-covered ropes that direct traffic in a museum, keep people where the museum directors want them to be. They are boundaries between visitors and the protected treasures. If you want to treasure yourself, you will want to place stanchions in your life as well.

Stanchions in your life will reduce incidents of people stepping inside your space without permission. Here are some common stanchions:

1. **Clear agreements with people**
   - "Now, I want to be very clear about what each of us is expecting in this arrangement."
   - "So, you're planning to be at the center at three o'clock sharp?"
   - "My understanding, then, is that you will be in charge of all aspects of the event except the food. Is that right?"

2. **Confident knowledge of yourself**
   - "No, that's not my style."
   - "No, I don't do well in those situations."
   - "I require less structure than you're suggesting. Can we compromise?"
   - "I work best when I am part of a team."

3. **Commitment to your goals**

- "I'm sorry, that just doesn't fit the direction I have chosen."

- "I have decided to forego that opportunity for now, but thank you."

- "I realize that I used to agree with you on this, but after giving it a lot of thought, I have changed my mind."

- "I have committed myself to using my lunch hour for a private retreat three times a week, but I'd love to schedule lunch with you every other Tuesday."

4. **An air of ownership**

- An appearance that says you are authentic and know what is appropriate

- Physical movement that shows intention

- Confidence in your role and contribution

- A spirit of enthusiasm and adventure

- A calm "knowing"

Stanchions are respectful boundary tools that let people know both who you are, and how they fit into your life. They reduce unwanted boundary violations, clearly show people what your limits are, and protect everyone from unnecessary misunderstandings.

Backup System

When the power goes off, or the wire is cut, the security backup system kicks in. To protect yourself well, you will want to install a backup power supply in your personal boundary system. It might include elements such as

1. **Promises to yourself**

- "When I reach a certain point of exhaustion or stress, I will stop, identify the problem, and/or get the rest or help I need."

- "When I feel pressured to make a decision, I will withdraw myself physically or mentally to regain my centeredness."

- "When I feel 'swallowed up' or controlled by another person, I will stop or redirect the encounter to reestablish my confidence in myself."

- "When I am rejected, I will feel the discomfort, sort through my part, if any, accept the current circumstances, learn, and move on."

- "When I am tempted to return to my addiction, I will stop instantly and resort to my backup plan to counter the temptation."

2. **On-call help**

   - A confidante: A person who can let you vent your feelings, rational or not, and not hold you to them later, or tell anyone else

   - A mentor: A person you admire and trust to encourage, teach, and guide you

   - A team of personal advisors: A group of experts, professional or not, who have your best interests in mind and have specific knowledge that can equip you

   - A short-notice pal: A person who can usually meet you for a quick meal or talk to you by phone at the drop of a dime

   - Creative rechargers: Books, movies, quotes, music, walks, flowers, delicacies, making something, a day away, pets, journaling, playing a game, revisiting your dreams, people watching, or visiting a favorite person with no agenda except company

   - Professionals who will try to "squeeze you in": Your hairstylist, masseuse, dry cleaner, florist, accountant, or mechanic

   - Helping team: Friends and family who will bail you out when a project goes sideways and you need help licking stamps, stapling brochures, setting up chairs, or delivering flowers

3. **Personal power sources**

- Physical: Massage, sleep, exercise, vitamins, good nutrition, or a hot tub

- Spiritual: Prayers you speak or read, inspirational reading from books or sacred text, meditation, affirmations, or visualization

- Emotional: Getting your feelings out, crying, laughing, yelling, venting in a way that is safe for you and others

- Mental: Thinking about something else for awhile, going to a bookstore in search of a new thought or alternative answer, creative problem-solving

Enforcement

When a visitor to a museum oversteps or violates the boundaries that have been established to protect the treasures, the enforcers take over. Depending on the infraction, the violator is stopped in whatever way is appropriate. Privileges as a guest are suspended, and the trespasser may be cuffed and carted away. When someone steps over the lines you have set, you will need to enforce your boundaries with action. This is how you are your own best friend. You take action to protect yourself. Here are some enforcement options you may want to use:

1. **Speak up**

- "No!"

- "I will not accept your behavior."

- "Get out."

- "I need to let you know how that hurt me."

- "I feel used by your actions."

- "You have overstepped your bounds."

2. **Suspend privileges**

- "Our relationship is off until further notice."

- "I will not continue in this arrangement."

- "Life as we've known it is on hold."

- "Let's step away from this and come back to it when we have adjusted our behavior."

3. **Withdraw**

   - Leave the scene physically.

   - Withdraw emotionally to keep your objectivity.

   - Stay away from the person, situation, location.

   - Retreat and start fresh.

4. **Denounce**

   - "You are no longer welcome here."

   - "I am drawing a line between you and me right now. You are not to cross it."

   - Refuse to speak about it anymore, hang up the phone, or send a registered letter. If appropriate, call for help, get a restraining order, hire an attorney, or dial 911.

Permission and Precautions

As you set up your personal boundary system, you should build in certain *permissions* and *precautions* to protect yourself:

- You are permitted and encouraged to readjust your boundaries as your personal beliefs about yourself and others change, and as you find out some things work better than others.

- You are permitted and encouraged to experiment with what works for you without concern about mistakes, judgments, or looking foolish. Take a "Hey, I'm learning" approach to your boundaries and to treasuring yourself.

- You are permitted and encouraged to value your opinions and choices enough to protect them.

- We caution you to install your personal boundary system discreetly and with the help of only your most trusted and good-spirited advocates.

How Your Personal Boundary System Works

Defines you. Your personal boundary system will identify what you will or will not allow into your life. You determine your lines and make your own choices. In other words, you are defined by your choices.

Lets good in and keeps bad out. How you define good and bad will be up to you. Our simple definition is: Good will honor, respect, and enhance you and your life. It will let in people, activities, beliefs, and choices that enrich you. Bad will dishonor, disrespect, or diminish you and your life. It will try to make you feel bad about yourself, hurt you, or threaten to control, manipulate, or take over your identity. As authors Milton Cudney and Robert Hardy write in their book *Self-Defeating Behaviors: Free Yourself from the Habits, Compulsions, Feelings, and Attitudes That Hold You Back,* "At each new moment in life people choose to behave in one of two ways: They opt for either a *self-defeating* or a *life-enhancing* behavior. Self-defeating behaviors are, essentially, any actions that separate the individual from his or her healthy core of attitudes, beliefs, feelings, and values. Life-enhancing behaviors, on the other hand, are actions or stances that either establish or affirm the individual's connection with his or her intact and life-giving essence."

Identifies who will get closest to you. There are those in a museum who get to be close to and, in some cases, handle the precious artifacts. They are beyond screening and stanchions and hidden cameras; instead, some of them know the alarm codes and operate the cameras. These people are the special, trusted ones. In your life you will invite some people to get very close to you, and of those, you will trust a few with special privileges. You feel safe with them, they are committed to your good as you are to theirs, and they enjoy who you are.

This process requires you to sort through the crowd, so to speak, and decide who's who in your life. Who will you love? Who will hear your secrets or get to listen to you sing at the top of your lungs on the backroads in a convertible? Who will watch you cry? Who will witness your accomplishments and listen to the details? Who will be your talking friends, your walking friends, or your shopping pals? Who will mentor you, influence your choices, or challenge your opinions? What criteria will you use to determine who's who?

The important thing is that you require yourself to walk the line between welcoming and trusting, and being cautious. You have a lot to protect, and caution is an important quality to own.

Personal Boundary Systems in Action

It is often helpful to watch others use their personal boundary system. Here are some case studies requiring boundary decisions.

Ted. Thirty-five-year-old Ted won a trip to Hawaii. He and his wife would finally get the honeymoon they had wanted since marrying seven years before. Ted called his wife to tell her the news, then reached for the phone to call his friend Henry.

As Ted was dialing, he remembered calling Henry with good news at other times and feeling disappointed by Henry's apparent lack of interest. Instead of letting the call go through, Ted chose to set a boundary between he and Henry—calling Henry would only perpetuate a negative pattern in their friendship. Ted decided not to sabotage his own excitement by calling a friend who he knew would bring him down. He disconnected the phone call in order to protect his feelings of happiness by waiting until later to call his friend.

If Ted's boundaries had been weak, he would have called Henry anyway, but it would have been out of obligation, not joy. The stress, sadness, and disappointment would have poured cold water on his joy. By waiting a few hours, Ted was able to fully share his happiness with friends who were happy for him, then call Henry and share the news without the need for an enthusiastic response.

Joanna. Joanna was offered a job by a company one thousand two hundred miles away. She was excited by the offer and by the increase in pay it would give her. Her first reaction was to say "yes" without asking more in-depth questions. Jumping into what appeared to be a good situation and then finding out it wasn't had been a damaging pattern Joanna had adopted earlier in her life. As part of her new commitment to caring for herself, she had installed a "stop-look-listen" screening process into making decisions.

First, she *stopped*. Joanna realized she was flattered by the job offer, and recognized her tendency to both commit too soon, and to be carried away by the fun of a possible new adventure.

She stepped away from those emotions to examine her old pattern, and chose to assess the situation before she acted.

Second, she *looked*. She considered all of the implications of the new job. What is the company culture, its reputation, the expectations that go with the pay hike, the location, the impact on her friendships and career, and the advancement potential?

Third, she *listened*. Joanna sought input from her team of advisors, friends and family, and professionals in her field. She read periodicals, resource information about the company and region, and articles on the effects of relocation. She also listened to her Self by spending time tapping into her intuition and spirit. She meditated and visualized about the move.

This screening process protected Joanna from a negative experience. The company turned out to be a difficult environment and was notorious for placing unreasonable demands on its middle managers. She refused the job offer without regrets.

Tim and Susan. Tim and Susan announced to Tim's parents that they were going to have a baby. The couple was hoping for a happy response. Instead, Tim's father groaned and his step-mother said, "I didn't sign up for this. I've had my children and I'm not a baby-sitter." When Tim's parents continued to display indifference, even after their grandson was born, Tim and Susan chose to protect more than their own hurt feelings about Tim's parents' negative response. They protected their baby by being selective about who shared in his life. They let good come to the baby from those who treasured him and kept bad out by limiting his exposure to the uninterested and dishonoring relatives.

If Tim and Susan had weak boundaries, they would have risked harming their child's emotions and their own feelings of well-being by continuing to present the child to the grandparents with predictable, negative results. Instead of yielding to an obligation to fulfill what normally would be perceived as their "duty" to their parents, they drew a line that protected and preserved their own family's good.

Gwen. One night while Gwen was sitting on the green sofa in her apartment listening to one of her favorite CDs, her boyfriend of seven months went into a rage, and instead of threatening to hit her as he often did, he actually did hit her. Gwen had dangerously chosen to let her boyfriend remain in her life even though he verbally abused her. She had put faith in the common belief that if she would do a better job of loving him, he would stop emotionally abusing her. When he did hit her, Gwen quickly installed an inflexible boundary between them both legally and personally. Although he tested her boundary for several weeks, he eventually gave up.

Gwen's story brings up some important points we would like to make about abuse and boundaries. First, love does not abuse. Selfishness and control abuse. Abusers choose to hurt others because it feeds a need for them to be in control, to exert power over another person. Second, if you are being abused, please seek qualified, professional help before setting new boundaries with your abuser. Because abuse is a control issue, abusers become alarmed when victims show signs of taking back control of their lives. Many times abuse will intensify when the victim takes a stand against the abuse. There are many helpful agencies and resources available to victims and their families, including the national domestic violence hotline at 1-800-799-SAFE. You may want to also read our book on the topic of abuse—*It's Not Okay Anymore, Your Personal Guide to Ending Abuse, Taking Charge, and Loving Yourself*. It is available through your local bookstore.

Reminding Yourself

- You already have a personal boundary system.

- Your active, connected system lovingly protects, preserves, and presents you.

- Your personal boundary system lets others know who you are, what you want, and what you can give.

- Your personal boundary system will include elements similar to a museum security system.

- Your boundary system essentials include signage, screening devices, alarms, guards, mirrors, recorders, stanchions, a backup system, and enforcement.

- Your boundary system will flexibly adjust to changing situations, beliefs, and circumstances.

4

The Guarantees and Challenges of Boundaries

The Guarantees of Boundaries

People who have refined their boundary-setting skills will tell you there are certain guarantees you can count on. Here are some of them:

- You will sometimes feel afraid and awkward.

- You will improve setting your boundaries with practice.

- Most people will adjust to your boundaries, like water parting for a stone.

- You will be blindsided or fooled by interlopers who appear to be good for you but aren't (it's happened to most people at least once).

- You will experience a new peace and calmness.

- Your life will be less cluttered and distracted.

- A sense of direction will emerge.

- You will have room to enjoy those people who enrich and inspire you.

- You will attract others with healthy boundaries.

- Friends who don't like your boundaries may lose interest.

- You will spend less time repairing your life and more time enhancing it.

- You will have less reason to retract, amend, feel guilty or embarrassed.

- You will have more energy and clarity.

- You will have more enthusiasm and hope.

- You will enjoy a new sense of control over your life.

- You will be more willing to take intelligent risks because you will know how to set limits to protect yourself.

- You will know how to respond to boundary violations.

- You will have more understanding and respect for other people's boundaries.

- You will experience increased creativity, excitement, and passion.

- You will have more time to spend with the people you love.

- You will come to believe that boundary-setting based on treasuredness is the most freeing skill you have ever learned.

The Challenges to Boundaries

No matter who you are or how well-defined your life is, your boundaries are challenged virtually every day. Everyone we know, however, who has an effective personal boundary system based on being their own best friend says surpassing the challenges is worth it, no matter how difficult. There is something wonderful and indescribable about owning and loving your life.

Here are some challenges faced by many people when creating boundaries:

Life Shifts

Life and relationships shift on you. Things are always moving and needing adjustments; opportunities and attitudes change;

what used to be isn't what's now, and new lines need to be drawn. You must decide when to say "yes," when to say "no," when to step in, when to keep out, when to leap, when to hold back, or when to speak up. These and other decisions are among the challenges, responsibilities, and privileges that both tax and rejuvenate you.

Disagreements

Boundaries are complicated also because your decision about where and when to install them is so personal. Your lines won't necessarily be drawn where your partner or friend or child would draw them. It's necessary, then, for you to build in honesty, discussion, and mutual respect as you create and maintain boundaries with those close to you. Once you have experienced this process, you will have both a new sense of freedom and ownership over your life.

Outside Opinions

Some people will find the very idea of you owning your life offensive. They believe claiming ownership is too bold, forceful, and selfish. Interestingly, they probably wouldn't feel this way if you were talking about owning your car. To say, "I own my car so I will make choices for it," seems logical and nonthreatening. Yet, for some to hear, "I own my life so I can make choices for it," sounds too arrogant, proud, and independent.

Misunderstandings

Your boundaries will be misunderstood, even by those close to you, and especially by those not particularly close to you. We guarantee it.

Common circumstances of misunderstandings. Misunderstandings occur most often when

- You have not adequately paved the way for your new boundary through respectful notification and discussion.

- The person involved has a weak boundary system and therefore cannot respect yours.

- The person involved is bent on controlling you.

- The person involved only supports your growth if it doesn't require him or her to make an adjustment.

Common sources of misunderstandings. The following list includes some of the most common misunderstandings:

- *Misunderstanding:* Boundaries are selfish.
  Truth: Boundaries are not selfish, in fact, they can actually open the door to more effective service to others. When you know and treasure yourself, you are better equipped with knowledge, time, and energy to love and give.

- *Misunderstanding:* Setting boundaries is self-centered gibberish and a waste of time.
  Truth: How deep you choose to look inside yourself is up to you, but it's truly important to look long enough to see what's standing between you and a positive, happy life.

- *Misunderstanding:* Setting boundaries makes relationships more difficult.
  Truth: Relationships are complicated anyway, but they can become a destruction derby without boundaries! The energy that could be applied toward a fun, stimulating relationship is often used up for repair work on relationships without boundaries. Plus, the experience of boundaried people in relationships is that boundary-setting opens the door to interesting and loving discussions. It also creates a new way to show respect for one another.

- *Misunderstanding:* Boundaries are just another pop psychology fad.
  Truth: Boundaries are as old as time. What may be new is discussing them over coffee with a friend. As a society, we are on a search for solutions to the mysteries of relationships, so naturally an interest in boundaries has developed since they are so essential to the success of personal interactions.

- *Misunderstanding:* Setting boundaries just doesn't work.
  Truth: If boundaries don't work, it is because they have been incorrectly or ineffectively installed. Having your boundaries challenged doesn't mean they aren't working—it means they are. In most cases, however, boundaries are an accepted, natural process in our universe. They work.

- *Misunderstanding:* Kind, giving, and loving people don't set boundaries.

  Truth: Some kind, giving, and loving people set boundaries; others don't. The ones who do are intentional and give because they want to, usually—their love stems from genuine interest. Those who don't set boundaries may also give out of a true desire to help. They often believe, however, that a "need constitutes a call," and feel guilty if they don't help, regardless of their emotional, physical, or financial condition. In the long run, givers without set boundaries burn out or have to quit giving to recover.

Self-Appointed Referees

There will be some in your life who will, to your face or not, call "foul" when you set a limit that stops them from diminishing, controlling, or discounting you. They will say things like, "Who does she think she is?" "I guess I'm not good enough for her anymore," "Since when can't he give up a day with his kid to be with me!" "She's into that 'boundaries' thing lately. It'll pass," or, "He used to be so nice and now, well, you know what I mean."

Excuses

There is a familiar set of excuses that may tempt you to postpone creating better boundaries. We suggest you admit to yourself from the start that there can be some fear associated with boundary-setting. We encourage you to feel the fear and do it anyway. Here are some common excuses for not setting boundaries:

- Our family has gotten along fine without them.

- I don't trust that psychological stuff.

- I just live day-to-day and trust that things will work out.

- It's easier to say "yes" than it is to say "no."

- If I set boundaries, I might as well kiss this relationship (job, friend, opportunity) goodbye.

- I'm already too tired. I don't need one more thing to do.

- People are used to me just like I am. They'd all go into shock if I changed now.

- I'm known for being a person who is always there and I'm not about to let anyone down.

- I have a friend who tried setting boundaries and people in her life couldn't take it.

- Boundaries go against everything I was taught as a child.

- If I say "no" I'll have to explain myself.

- I'd like to change but everyday responsibilities just keep getting in the way.

- Boundaries are a luxury I can't afford.

- Boundaries are a good thing, I'm just not capable of making drastic changes.

Your Own Beliefs and Patterns

Not all challenges to your boundaries will come from outside yourself. Many will come from inside—where you think, feel, and make choices. We explain this more in later chapters. In the meantime, we want to prepare you for the inevitable: resistance from within.

This resistance will come in the form of misbeliefs, addictions, thinking errors, and defenses. You adopted these patterns to protect yourself during a time of pain or discomfort and continued to use them when the pain and discomfort were gone. They are "clutter" in your being, and they will fight to stay right where they are until you, as the owner of your life, step in and remove them. This book will help you to clean out the clutter.

Remember that building boundaries is a process. Being gentle with yourself through these changes is the only way to get past the resistance—maintain your sense of humor, and ask for help from those you admire and trust. Free yourself from blocks to personal power. Think to yourself, "I'm declaring war on my own bad habits!"

Fear

Change is scary because it takes you somewhere you've never been before. Fear's job is to alert you and even protect you from potential dangers and threats. Let fear do its job as the notifier and you do your job as the decider. When it stops you in your tracks, hear and value fear's message, act on it if necessary, and then dismiss it or go around it.

Ignorance

Another challenge to successful boundary-setting can be ignorance. If you don't know how to do something, you can't do it well. As so many have said, "Knowledge is power." This doesn't mean power over someone else; rather, it means power to understand and complete what it is you want to do. Fight ignorance with knowledge and experience. You live at a time when knowledge comes in endless forms, so choose the way you want to learn and become efficient on the subject of setting personal limits. Talk to people who say "yes" and "no" confidently; observe boundary issues in books, movies, and on television; listen to the way people state their boundaries; and experiment.

Facing the Challenge

The secret of breaking past a challenge is that once you get past it, it gives you a prize. The prize is a boost in your opinion of yourself, in your sense of competence. This boost fuels you for the next challenge, which fuels you for the next, and on it goes.

We have noted that when people are asked about their most memorable event, they often name an achievement that stretched them beyond where they thought they could go. People have a yearning to expand themselves, but they often lack the courage, support, will, or heart to do what's necessary. They are often forced into pushing themselves further by an upsetting life circumstance that demands making a decision to act. Challenge is what you crawl over to reach what you want, and like we said, challenge offers great reward to those who conquer it.

Reminding Yourself

- There are certain built-in guarantees to creating better boundaries.

- You can expect your boundary-setting to be challenged from a number of sources, including yourself.

- There will be some who are bent on violating your boundaries.

- Facing and surpassing the challenges increases your sense of competence, and therefore your self-esteem.

- No one with effective boundaries regrets going to the trouble of creating them.

Part II

Treasuring Yourself

5

Becoming Your Own Best Friend

The shortest route to better boundaries is to really like yourself. Better yet, really love yourself. Eileen is a spirited, loving friend who is the first to admit things about herself that need improving. Still, her attitude is "I always assume people will be as glad to see me as I am to see them. Why shouldn't they be?" Eileen sees herself as a terrific person with areas that need adjusting, not a flawed person with some good qualities. Rabbi Harold Kushner, author of *How Good Do I Have to Be?* would commend Eileen. He says, "When we let ourselves be defined in our own minds by our worst moments instead of our best ones, we learn to think of ourselves as people who never get it right, rather than as capable people who make an occasional, thoroughly human mistake." How do you see yourself?

The process of treasuring involves learning to befriend yourself—to become your own best friend and treat yourself as a treasure like the ruby slippers. When you befriend yourself, you watch out for yourself and plan a life you would want your most treasured friend to live, and then protect your life with boundaries that work to keep the bad out and let the good in. In a real sense, befriending yourself is establishing an honest and rewarding relationship with yourself. After all, a person naturally takes good care of what he or she treasures.

Basic Elements

The process of learning to treasure yourself will include these basic elements:

1. Declare yourself to be the owner of your life and your own best friend.

2. Look at what you believe about yourself and what opinions you hold.

3. Sort out what is true and what is not; work on keeping what is, toss what's not.

4. Get to know your true self.

5. Continue to adjust your conclusions about yourself based on what is true.

6. Set and adjust your boundaries.

7. Live the treasured life.

Have you experienced relationships where you were truly treasured, where you felt safe and cherished, knew you were free, and felt you were both able to express yourselves fully? This is a great experience, especially when one of your treasured relationships is with yourself. Sadly, this is not most people's experience, which is more in line with author Joe Tye's book *Personal Best*. He writes, "More often than not, we don't want to know ourselves, don't want to depend on ourselves, don't want to live with ourselves. By middle life, most of us are accomplished fugitives from ourselves."

Rather than escape from yourself, become your own best friend and create a safe place for yourself to thrive. Realize that no matter what, you will not cast yourself out of your own heart. When you befriend yourself, you gain a built-in buddy who treasures you, watches out for you, cheers you on, comforts you, and keeps you company. This adds a rich and calming dimension to your life. Instead of worrying that you will sabotage your own happiness, you know you will be your own best friend.

The whole notion of being valuable—a priceless, unique treasure, not unlike the ruby slippers—is essential in the practice of setting and maintaining healthy, respectful boundaries. To some, the idea of treasuring yourself may seem unattainable, reserved for an elite few; to others, it may seem like an unnecessary, frivolous pursuit. Developing and maintaining love for yourself is both attainable and near. It results in an enthused, endlessly interesting life you won't want to miss.

Befriending yourself is not an event, it's a lifestyle. Like any prized relationship, you will keep it alive with attention, honesty, and communion. As M. Scott Peck writes in *The Road Less Traveled*, "When we love something it is of value to us, and when something is of value to us we spend time with it, time enjoying it, and time taking care of it." The same is true when you love yourself. The process of becoming your own best friend contains the elements of any positive, life-building relationship. You meet, gradually learn about each other, develop trust, cultivate honesty, share life and dreams, and forgiveness. You guard one another's good, and you help each other. Lasting relationships develop a richness over time and create a unique rhythm and design.

Owning Your Life

When your name is on the title of a car, you own it. It would be helpful if each of us were given a similar title to our lives to prove they belong to us, too. In fact, you may want to write out a title to your life and keep it with you, or frame it. Such a gesture would notify and remind you, and others, that nobody else but you has the right to "drive" your life without your permission. That, of course, is the essence of the challenge of boundaries.

When you own a car, you have the last word in who gets to drive it, for how long, how far, at what time, and where. You may or may not be an effective owner of the car. You may take a laissez-faire attitude, believing that somehow the automobile will be just fine without you having to pull rank as the owner. Or, you may take a controlling approach and keep even trusted people from enjoying it. Or, you may take a more balanced approach and settle for somewhere in between these two possibilities.

The key point to understand is that if you are a careless or timid owner of your life, other people—well- and not so well-meaning—will slip behind the wheel and take you to places you may not want to go. If, on the other hand, you are an overbearing owner of your life, you will lock the car doors and keep anyone from going along for a free ride. A smart owner will stay behind the wheel, invite some to ride along, but not others. If you treasure yourself, you will go places that stimulate, challenge, and delight. You will be able to look back on the "trip," with the pride of an owner of a Mercedes that's successfully traveled three hundred thousand miles on the same engine.

A sense of ownership is essential to both treasuring yourself and setting boundaries. So, if you've let your sense of ownership get a little sloppy, stop now and take back the keys to your life. Do what you have to do to make the transaction real to you. Here are some suggestions:

- On a paper, or in the margins of this book, print your name. Under your printed name, write your signature, followed by the word "Owner."

- Run a movie in your head. You're the star and you're rescuing yourself from the rule of others, taking back your life from their control. You go from person to person, circumstance to circumstance, and take yourself back to a safe place.

- Create an "ownership statement," such as "I own my life and make good, caring choices for it." Memorize it. Use it. Live it.

- Frame and display an appropriate photo, card, or item to remind you of your decision to own your life.

Congratulations! You are the owner of a shiny, special limited edition Life!

Naming Your Motives

Why be your own best friend? The main reason is to assure yourself the best care possible. Who's better qualified to know what you need than you? While it's vital to have intimate friends to help you grow and thrive, it's also in your best interest to learn to trust and enjoy yourself as an intimate friend who is devoted to your own good and fulfillment.

The following is a list of motives to reclaim ownership of your life:

- To be sure you get the care you need

- To control and direct your life
- To seize opportunities that excite you
- To cultivate your spoken and unspoken dreams
- To be a friend who depends on yourself, not others, for fulfillment
- To choose activities and experiences that strengthen your purpose
- To enjoy fully the privileges and responsibilities of ownership

What are your motives for owning your life?

_____

_____

_____

_____

_____

_____

_____

_____

_____

_____

Making Mind Shifts

Setting boundaries because you own your life and treasure yourself requires a wonderful blend of mind shifts and life adjustments. It is a process that puts you in charge of your life and permits you to direct it. The blend of mind shifts and life adjustments work together, one fueling the other. Soon you notice you are thinking in new ways and making new choices. This changes your life for the better, producing the momentum and appetite to continue the treasuring and boundary-setting process.

Maya Angelou, in her book *The Heart of a Woman*, includes a scene of her life in Cairo that we feel illustrates the process of setting new boundaries based on a mind shift toward treasured-ness. She had just arrived in Cairo with her teenaged son, Guy, to live with her new husband, African freedom fighter Vusumzi Make. Mr. Make had arrived sometime earlier to conduct business and prepare their home. He eagerly walked Maya and her son through room after room of satin sofas, tapestries, exquisite par-quetry, French antique furniture, outsized beds, and luxurious armoires. Maya believed the furnishings were rented. When she discovered her husband had purchased them, she said, "You mean, we own all that crap?" Her unexpected response hurt and an-gered both her husband and her son, and they left the room. As she stood there alone, she realized that her words were rooted in a belief that such furnishings and luxury were for white people, not her.

She describes her shift (one that we have interpreted as an example of a mind shift) this way: "A profound sense of worth-lessness had made me pull away from owning good things, ex-pensive furniture, rare rugs. That was exactly how white folks wanted me to feel. I was black, so obviously I didn't deserve to have armoires, shiny with good French veneer, or tapestries, where mounted warriors waged their ancient battles in silk thread. No, I decided to crush that feeling of unworthiness. I deserved every-thing beautiful and I merited putting my long black feet on Ori-ental carpets as much as Lady Astor."

Maya's decision to "crush that feeling of unworthiness" is a superb example of the process of a mind shift from not treasuring to treasuring Self. It likely resulted in a permanent change in her beliefs, leading to choices that allowed new beauty into her life without a debilitating sense of guilt or shame. She opened her boundaries to let "good" in, deciding to draw a line against her own false beliefs about what she deserved.

The harmful things we keep out of our lives don't always come from the people, situations, and things outside ourselves; we have many boundary violators living in our own minds in the form of beliefs and opinions about ourselves, others, and the world. The more you reject these misleading beliefs and opinions, the more mind shifts you will experience. Ms. Angelou cooper-ated with her true inner voice by rejecting her false beliefs about what she could and could not own as a black woman. She accel-erated her process of mind-shifting authentication by being open to new truth when it hit her. In this way, she was acting as her own best friend.

Treasuring Is a Process

We have referred to treasuring yourself and setting effective boundaries as a "process." For some, the word "process" automatically triggers resistance, especially if it's dubbed a "lifelong process." If you have difficulty mustering enthusiasm for something that continues until you die, change the way you think of it. Imagine the process as stepping on a lifestyle path that will take you to beautiful places. Or, picture it as an upward spiral, with each step lifting you to the next. However you choose to see it, each step is a goal accomplished, a win that motivates you to the next win. It's like rolling doubles in Monopoly. You get another chance to win the game.

Feeling discouraged by the thought of a lengthy process is like a dieter who is told it will take five months to lose extra weight. Then, when the first few pounds are lost, he or she remembers that the rewards of even long-term processes begin immediately. With learning better boundaries, the small goals can invigorate you and motivate you toward a bigger goal. Each step is a win for you and will spur you forward toward your goal of successfully managing your life. Simply reading this chapter, or taking a small action like limiting the number of times you agree to something you can't comfortably do today, is a success in boundary-setting. Remember, treasuring yourself is the finest gift you could give yourself, the people you love, and the world that needs your authentic contribution.

Reminding Yourself

- Being your own best friend is a quick way to create better boundaries.

- Claiming, or reclaiming, ownership of your life is essential to treasuring yourself and setting boundaries that work to keep the bad out and let the good in.

- The motivation for being your own best friend is to assure yourself the best care possible, therein building a foundation for sustained success in personal happiness.

- Treasuring and owning your life requires mind shifts.

- Becoming your own best friend and owner of your life is an ongoing process.

6

Knowing What You
Think about Yourself

Your existing boundaries are a result of what you think about
yourself. Your opinion of yourself is built on all of the information
you have gathered since birth. In this chapter, we will help you
realize how much or little you value yourself. Becoming aware
of your sense of self-worth will help you to recognize what types
of personal boundaries you need to develop.

The best motive for setting boundaries is simply to value
yourself enough to *protect* yourself from harm, *preserve* yourself
for fulfillment, and *present* yourself for service. This is the essence
of befriending yourself, and it requires an ongoing awareness of
what beliefs are influencing your choices.

Recognizing Treasured Thinking

What do people who treasure themselves believe about themselves? It is important that you know so that you can have
something to compare your beliefs to. The following belief statements summarize the foundation of treasured thinking. Rate how
strongly each belief matches your own.

A = Definitely True

B = Mostly True

C = Somewhat True

D = Not Very True

E = Hardly True, If At All

1. I have the power to make choices   A B C D E
   for myself.

2. I am both valuable and imperfect.   A B C D E

3. I am in a lifelong process of growth.   A B C D E

4. My individual significance is not lowered A B C D E
   or raised by others' opinions of me.

5. My life is enriched when living in   A B C D E
   interdependent relationships with
   cooperative and respectful people.

6. My life is diminished when living   A B C D E
   in interdependent relationship with
   uncooperative and disrespectful people.

7. My instrinsic, or built-in, value is neither A B C D E
   more nor less than other people's.

8. Certain types of contributions will   A B C D E
   be more esteemed than others in
   our society or circle, but this does
   not add to or diminish the significance
   of my contribution.

9. Others' talents are a pleasure to observe A B C D E
   and applaud.

10. I value life and operate from a sense of   A B C D E
    gratitude, not entitlement.

11. I am able to face challenges and   A B C D E
    meet problems.

12. I accept and befriend myself.   A B C D E

13. I believe I contribute significantly   A B C D E
    to the good of others and the world.

14. It is my right and privilege to own   A B C D E
    my feelings.

15. Boundaries are necessary and   A B C D E
    appropriate.

16. Boundaries do not violate love.   A B C D E

17. Setting limits is necessary to keep   A B C D E
    relationships healthy and vital.

18. I am not compelled to justify a   A B C D E
    boundary with apologetic explanations.

The level of friendliness you have for yourself will be the foundation for the boundaries you build in your life. This can be pictured using the *Beliefscape* below. Simply fill in the column above the number of each question to the letter you circled for that question. For example, if you circled the letter "B" on Belief #1, then fill in that column up through the letter "B." If you circled the letter "E" on Belief #2, then you would fill in only the "E."

Leon, a loving man in his forties, whose relationship with his second wife was ending, completed this *Beliefscape*. It revealed a common dilemma. While Leon believed "boundaries are necessary and appropriate," and marked it "A=Definitely True," he quickly saw that he had difficulty applying them in key areas of his life because he felt selfish setting limits.

The *Beliefscape* became Leon's map for building better boundaries.

Leon's Beliefscape

	1	2	3	4	5	6	7	8	9	10	11	12	13	14	15	16	17	18
A = Definitely True																		
B = Mostly True																		
C = Somewhat True																		
D = Not Very True																		
E = Hardly True, If at All																		

Picturing Your Beliefs

Now it's your turn. To picture what you believe about yourself, your treasuredness, and your right to set boundaries, transfer your belief ratings to the *Beliefscape*.

The goal is to believe so strongly in your value that your *Beliefscape* is fully colored in so the foundation of your life can be solid and level, ready for boundary-setting. It can be done. Picturing your beliefs this way helps you see (1) the *strength* or *depth* of your positive self-view, (2) the overall *stability* of your beliefs about your value, and (3) the *need* for your beliefs to be adjusted. As your sense of treasuredness increases, so will the stability of your boundaries.

What if your *Beliefscape* shows that your sense of treasuredness is quite strong, yet your boundaries are weak? At least two things could cause this, (1) you feel friendly toward yourself but don't know how to set boundaries; or, (2) you have not been truthful about your real beliefs about yourself.

Knowing What You Think of Yourself Right Now

Using the *Beliefscape* exercise, you have rated your beliefs about your self-worth, or treasuredness. Now it's time to look at how you view yourself in relation to others.

A jump-start to identifying how you view yourself right now is to select opinions that strike you as true. From those words, you can then form a sentence that summarizes how you view yourself. From the following list, please check those words or phrases that most authentically express what you believe about yourself today. Try to go beyond what you *want* to believe or think you *should* believe, and mark what you *really* believe. Add any words or phrases that apply to you but are missing from the list.

Opinion Words

Attractive	Awkward	Clumsy
Competent	Confident	Creative
Damaged goods	Deserving	Destined for failure
Determined	Devoted	Dorky

Your Beliefscape

How well do your beliefs about your treasuredness support your life?

	1	2	3	4	5	6	7	8	9	10	11	12	13	14	15	16	17	18
A = Definitely True																		
B = Mostly True																		
C = Somewhat True																		
D = Not Very True																		
E = Hardly True, If at All																		

Dreamer	Fearful	Fearless
Flawed	Focused	Fun
Funny	Growing	Hardworking
Humorless	Incompetent	Innovative
Insightful	Intelligent	Intentional
Inventive	Invisible	Loser
Lovable	Loving	Mute
Naive	No good	Overlooked
Passionate	Persevering	Persuasive
Powerful	Powerless	Promising
Resourceful	Self-assured	Slow
Stuck	Successful	Talented
Unable to succeed	Unattractive	Undeserving
Unlovable	Valuable	_____
_____	_____	_____
_____	_____	_____
_____	_____	_____
_____	_____	_____
_____	_____	

Your Opinion Statement

Use the words or phrases you have checked to create your opinion statement. This differs from an identity, or mission, statement because it is your *opinion*, and your opinions of yourself may or may not be true to your identity and mission. The goal eventually, though, is to more accurately align opinions of yourself with your identity.

For example, Leon's opinion statement, now that he has adjusted his beliefs about himself, might read: "In my opinion, I am competent, growing, promising, focused, loving, persuasive, and determined."

Another woman, Julie, who struggles with setting limits on the amount of time she spends on the phone with friends who call for encouragement, had the following opinion statement: "In my opinion, I am nice, helpful, loving, insightful, powerless to say 'no,' and undeserving of time to myself."

Using the opinion words or phrases you selected from the list, and any others you added, create an opinion statement of your own.

"In my opinion, I am _____

_____

_____

_____ ."

Identifying Other Opinions
You Have about Yourself

Another revealing exercise is to examine targeted opinions about yourself. This exercise increases your awareness in specific areas, helping you to evaluate your overall friendliness toward yourself. This exercise also calls attention to parts of yourself you feel very good or very bad about. It's not at all uncommon to be surprised by at least one opinion you have about yourself. Read this list to better understand your self-view. Perhaps the list will trigger you to think about areas of your life not highlighted in these exercises. What opinions do you hold about:

Your competence _____

Your lovability _____

Your performance at work _____

Your looks _____

Your personal disciplines _____

Your friendliness _____

Your intelligence _____

Your strengths _____

Your weaknesses _____

Your reputation _____

Your skills _____

Your ability to cope with stress _____

Reminding Yourself

- You now know what kinds of beliefs people who treasure themselves hold.

- Your self-beliefs support your boundary-setting.

- You can become aware of, and adjust, general, or specific, opinions you hold about yourself.

7

Understanding the Source and Strength of Your Self-Beliefs

Can you imagine if every word, action, impression, insinuation, and look you ever received clung to you like a barnacle clings to a ship? This is actually pretty close to the truth. What you've gathered about yourself from other people and life so far has contributed to your self-view. It's true that some things have held on more tightly than others, but most experts agree that in one way or another, things stick until you cut them free. Richard Brodie, in his book *Getting Past OK: A Straightforward Guide to Having a Fantastic Life*, says, "Beliefs or attitudes learned in the past can be like training wheels never removed from a bicycle, hindering us in improving our quality of life."

Tracing the Sources of Your Self-Beliefs

The strongest opinions you hold about yourself are those you formed at home, with your parents or primary caregivers. Like most children, you probably adopted the spoken and unspoken beliefs of your family. These beliefs have been with you the longest and are the toughest to adjust. With each passing year, your opinions deepened from other influences like relatives, teachers, friends, authority figures, books, media, and circumstances.

Your opinion of yourself is a result of not only what has been said and done to you, but also the way you have interpreted what has been said and done to you. Over time, your self-beliefs and conclusions became your identity, therefore, your life choices and boundaries grew from your identity.

It's pretty easy to spot parental impact on our view of ourselves, life, and the world. The following are two profiles to illustrate this.

Mickey's father is particularly cynical toward television news anchors, weather forecasters, and basically anyone officially dispensing information. Mickey grew up hearing his father accompany the news with a nonstop sarcastic grumble. "Yeah, I wonder who's paying this station off—just tell me the news, jerk, don't interpret it for me." Mickey adopted his father's attitude, and, as an adult, he would become tense during the news and would hear himself making similar remarks. His contempt for experts led him to close himself off from engaging discussion of the news and ideas, shutting down any openness to new outside thoughts.

In contrast, Natalie grew up in a home where thoughts and ideas were hotly and enjoyably debated over dinner. Everyone got to have their own opinion and defend it without worrying that disagreeing opinions would result in damaged relationships. The family's favorite television shows centered around biographies, discoveries, and documentaries. They loved commenting on the news.

Natalie's life includes rich experience and a textured worldview because of her experience at home. Mickey isn't quite as receptive to an open-minded worldview as a result of his father's influence.

One part of responsible life ownership is sorting through the opinions and beliefs that have shaped and motivated you. You can clear out the ones that keep you from treasuring yourself and others, owning your life, and setting effective boundaries. This will simplify boundary-setting because you will base your decisions on intentional, conscious beliefs rather than on a complex compendium of unconscious and undesired influences.

"Labels" You May Have Received

If you are curious about where your opinion of yourself and the world began, look at the opinion statement you created in chapter 6. As best you can, trace each opinion word back to its origins. If you are like most people, you will recall many of the voices and attitudes that shaped your opinions and identity. This is a helpful trip back in time that can be amusing, painful, inspiring, surprising, and sometimes embarrassing. Tracing your opinion statement puts faces and dates on your beliefs, making it a little easier to make choices about whether to keep or discard them.

Richard, a designer, did this using his opinion statement. The opinion words he had selected were "sissy, work below my potential, spacey, artistic, and dreamer." When he traced the words back to their source, here is what he discovered:

The Origins of Richard's Opinion Statement

Opinion Word	Who Said It	The Context of the Labeling
Sissy	Dad, older brother, and his friends	Dad and brother were award-winning athletes who teased me about my size and lack of interest in sports.
Works below potential	Teachers	Math teacher's comments on my report card.
Spacey	Teachers, parents	At parent-teacher conferences my parents and teachers described me as a spacey kid; and my parents nicknamed me "space cadet."
Artistic	Art teachers, friends, experts	My art teacher liked my work and I always got "A's." My friends were always wanting me to draw them pictures. A professional artist even encouraged me to enter some of my work in a show and I won first prize in the amateur division.
Dreamer	Grandmother, English teacher	Grandmother used to tell me, "Dreamers don't get anywhere, and you're a dreamer. Get your head out of the clouds, dear." My English teacher told me that I was a dreamer with a great imagination. He also told me my creative writing was "rich."

Like Richard, you may want to trace the words in your opinion statement on the chart below:

The Origins of Your Opinion Statement		
Opinion Word	Who Said It	The Context of the Labeling

Identifying Family Influences

As you traced the words of your opinion statement back to their sources, you may have noticed that your family had a lot to do with what you think of yourself. At least they were instrumental in getting you started toward particular self-beliefs. Much like a club, or team, a group living under the same roof often lives out an "enactment story." Author and psychiatrist Eric Berne was one of the first to describe these stories as "scripts." Scripts can be recognized by what a family says and how it behaves. It is from this script, and the roles people play, that many of your opinions and beliefs about yourself and your value emerged. According to Eric Berne, each of us has a script that tells us how to live out our lives. Yours was written for you by influential people like your parents, relatives, friends, teachers, and others. It's as if you were told, "Here's your script. Go live it." Scripts are open to rewrites, however, and you've probably rewritten yours to one degree or another based on other people's impressions, expectations, observations, and agendas, as well as your own. This happens on the conscious and unconscious level.

It is worth your time to identify the family scripts that influenced you. In her book *Family Interfaces: Transgenerational Patterns*, Dr. Jeannette Kramer writes, "Bringing the rules into conscious awareness is important because, when they are known, the individual can decide if he wants to follow them or not; if not, she can then decide how to change a rule for herself."

Embedded within scripts are rules and codes. What were the spoken and unspoken, positive and negative codes that your family lived by? You may want to write them on the lines following this list. We've supplied you with some tried and true codes to help you begin identifying those within your own family:

- "You always have enough to give to someone who has less."

- "Talk is cheap."

- "Never ask a stranger for help."

- "Naps in the middle of the day are for lazy people."

- "Avoid conflict at all costs."

- "Give people a chance."

- "Give people a chance and they'll screw you."

- "Don't take handouts."
- "Don't be afraid of failing, be afraid of not trying."
- "You can do anything you set your mind to."
- "Dreaming is for rich people."

Your Family's Spoken and Unspoken Rules

This is what was OKAY: **This is what was NOT OKAY:**

_____   _____

_____   _____

_____   _____

_____   _____

_____   _____

_____   _____

_____   _____

_____   _____

_____   _____

_____   _____

_____   _____

_____   _____

_____   _____

Family codes have a profound influence on us. Each new generation is significantly influenced by the previous generation's scripts; the struggles you face today have probably been passed down to you as an unintentional inheritance, so to speak. In the worst cases, one generation victimizes the next; in the best cases they create legacies of devotion, protection, mentoring, and celebration.

The good news is you can rewrite the scripts you've been given. You can improve the inheritance no matter how wonderful or awful it is. If you grew up in a family where you weren't—or perceived you weren't—treasured, you can now begin to say "no" to those dishonoring opinions. If you were fortunate enough to grow up in a family that helped you believe in your value, you will have a head start in owning your life and building boundaries upon a sense of personal worth. Most of us have had a mix of honoring and dishonoring input.

Andrew. Andrew's family had a script that said, "If you don't get good grades, you're dumb and won't amount to anything in life." A hard worker, but not a gifted student, Andrew struggled to pass his classes, but schoolwork wasn't his only struggle. He also struggled with his father's opinion of him. Based on Andrew's performance in school, his father, a businessman, would often tell his son, "You'll never amount to anything. You'll be lucky to get a job pumping gas."

Andrew barely graduated from high school. He publicly declared he would not pump gas, but he was secretly afraid his father's prediction for him would come true. As Andrew scanned his options, he decided to try to become a realtor. He liked the thought of helping people find just the right home. But there were tests to be taken, lots of them, and Andrew repeatedly failed them. His father's curse hung over Andrew's life until he finally did pass his realtor's exam.

Andrew never became a great scholar. His talents were in other areas. What he did become is a dynamic and highly successful commercial real estate professional by his midtwenties. Even with the evidence of success—a devoted wife, healthy kids, many friends, a rich spiritual life, and lots of money—Andrew still had to fight his role in the family script. To Andrew's credit, he dumped the old script and, with the help of trusted friends and occasional visits to a counselor, he shifted his thinking of himself as a failure to a success. Andrew came to realize (1) his strengths are not in the areas of reading and writing, and (2) he is very talented and gifted in the areas of communication, strategizing, and sales. As a result, Andrew created a new self-view that said, "I have never been a failure, though I have failed to reach certain academic objectives. Like everyone else, I have strengths and weaknesses, and my path for success will be in the area of my strengths." You too can adjust your self-beliefs and anchor your boundaries to the truth of your treasuredness.

Relatives

Your self-view may have also been influenced by your extended family, your grandparents, aunts, uncles, cousins, and step-families. Extended family is famous for labeling and nick-naming the next generation: "She's our entertainer," "He's our shy one," "Meet Scooter, he's always on the go," "He got the brains in the family." This ritual is usually meant as an endearing term of belonging, yet it often traps children into feeling obligated to an identity that may or may not be accurate. With a label usually comes a role to play. The little entertainer must entertain whether she feels like it or not, the shy boy must act shy, Scooter must stay busy, and the slow or the brainy one must live up to their designated titles. The choice is to either play the role or lose the seat in the family gallery of personalities. Most people are able to withstand a lifelong obligation to their assigned roles, but many find they are still influenced by these childhood expectations. What influence did your relatives have on creating your self-view?

_____

_____

_____

_____

_____

Recognizing Other Influencers

Teachers

We often help clients overcome the invalid labels that teachers gave them as children. Liz is an example of this. She is a professional watercolor artist who was told by her second grade teacher during an art project that she "would obviously never be an artist." The internal boundaries of a seven-year-old usually cannot block the opinions of authorities; therefore, Liz let this lie enter her belief system. For twenty-five years she avoided artistic expression, even though it violated her inner need to be creative. This false opinion of herself was exposed in the process of sorting through other misconceptions. Liz became free to explore the disparity between her deep desire to paint pictures and her complete conscious shut-down toward being an artist.

Not only does Liz's story serve as a wake-up call to carefully choose our statements to children, it also proves people can be helped to get past their false beliefs, to an authentic expression of who they are.

Liz and millions of other adults around the world get past their limiting self-beliefs every day. You can take the considerable energy you have been spending on living in a false role and re-direct it toward discovering and expressing your true identity in your life.

We want to pass along this inspiring example of a teacher's influence. Author Howard Clinebell, in his book *Wellbeing*, describes how he suffered "miserably" from low self-esteem and shyness. As a child, he began to tell himself, "I am slow and perhaps stupid." In turn, this belief caused him to present himself as less capable than he really was. "It was not until my second year in high school that I began to pull out of this intellectual tailspin. A social studies teacher who was excited about teaching modern history took an interest in this shy, awkward, pimply-faced teenager. He affirmed my mind by challenging me to read, think, discuss, and write down my thoughts. I sensed that he believed I could do this and do it well. To my surprise, I began to discover that I enjoyed and could in fact excel in intellectual pursuits. I shall always be profoundly grateful for that teacher. He enabled me gradually to revise my negative self-image, enjoy using my mind, and gain a sense of my real inner strength."

What influence did your teachers have on creating your self-view?

_____

_____

_____

_____

_____

Other Adults

Coaches, friends of the family, role models, clergy, baby-sitters, neighbors, and school mentors, can all be adult influencers that help form your self-view. As a child, your "life-map" was uncharted, and a parade of people became reference marks for your identity. The first milkman became the forerunner of all milkmen, and your mother's supervisor became the first image of a "boss." Others have followed, leaving their mark on your life, confirming or challenging your beliefs about yourself.

We have been writing this book in Jan's home to protect ourselves from interruptions at the office. Her house, a stucco cottage built in the forties, sits across the corner from a blue colonial. When we complete a draft, we sit in the living room to read and edit aloud. From the living-room window, we can see a wonderful example of adult influences happening at the blue colonial. Erin, a nanny, is affecting Cloey, six, and Susanna, three. Since birth, the girls' parents have encouraged them to express themselves creatively. Erin reinforces the parents' wish to honor the girls' individuality. There is an endless stream of discoveries, make-believe, and proclamations, such as announcements tacked to trees, "Cloey has lost a tooth," or "Hand-painted notecards for sale here."

A few mornings ago, Cloey, dressed in brown boots, daisy-covered turquoise shorts, a pajama top with a kitty on it, and a helmet, climbed out her side window on a mission to inspect the rhododendrons. In her hand was a striped umbrella. As she inspected, she twirled it, treating our eyes to the simple beauty of black and white spinning against the greens. Later, young Susanna marched onto the lawn and marched circles around Erin, banging a drum in her blue satin costume with stiff petticoats slipping out from under. Erin respectfully gives the girls space, instinctively knowing when to cuddle, when to discipline, and when to distance. Her honoring, creative attention will contribute to a lasting legacy of positive self-view. Erin allows the girls to develop independence, individuality, and an imagination.

Not all adult influences have the type of positive impact Erin has provided, but when they do, there is reason to celebrate.

What influence did other adults have on your self-view?

_____

_____

_____

_____

_____

Peers

It's no news to you that your peers influence your beliefs about yourself. They did when you were young, and they do now. Around adolescence, peer influence can be greater than any other. Ralph, an electrician, recently discovered why he was unwilling to return pop cans to the grocer. When he was thirteen, a group of his peers saw him redeeming cans at the store and labeled him "poor white trash." Ralph equated pop can redemption with this image and never again returned cans for cash, even though people of every economic level turn in their pop cans. Richard Brodie, in his book *Getting Past OK: A Straightforward Guide to Having a Fantastic Life*, recalls the influence of peers as a child, "If some of our beliefs were as visible as training wheels, we would see a lot quicker when the time came to let go of them. As I grew up, an overweight loner among the neighborhood kids, I learned people were not to be trusted. When boys would approach me, it was often to insult me or beat me up. I learned quickly to harden myself, to avoid eye contact, to ignore taunts. Although the severe hositility of that environment lasted only through junior high school, and in fact I met many people since then who wanted to be close to me, I rode around through life with the 'training wheels' of my distrust for a long time after that." What influence did your peers have on creating your self-view?

_____

_____

_____

_____

_____

Media, Entertainment, and Advertising

The impact of these three influencers on our self-view is immeasureable. They have sculpted new personal, community, and cultural standards that, for the most part are what even Oprah Winfrey called in an interview with *Life* magazine "false standards." Television, movies, music, the Internet, video games, and print media flood us with images that challenge our personal image. It takes strength to withstand this barrage of suggestion, comparisons, and artificial fulfillment with intentional, concentrated choices.

What influence has the entertainment industry had on creating your self-view?

_____

_____

_____

_____

_____

Defining Circumstances

There were significant events in your life that led you to conclude certain opinions about yourself. This was true particularly as you compared them to the circumstances of others' lives. Circumstances such as natural disasters, sickness, deaths, births, accidents, awards, marriages, divorces, losing a job, promotions, relocations, career choices, and the certain ways you were treated, just to name a few, furnished you with plenty of materials to mold your opinon of yourself.

For example, Doreen's father committed suicide when Doreen was five, and for a long time she believed she was bad and the cause of her father's suicide. This traumatic circumstance led Doreen to a false self-belief about her power over others. Doreen felt guilty for other people's pain, even though it wasn't her responsibility.

Gregory always felt inferior to his older brother who was a straight-A student. But in high school, Gregory earned two medals, one gold, at the museum science fair. This win altered his conclusion about his intellectual ability and became a positive benchmark in his self-esteem.

What influence have some of the defining circumstances of your life had on creating your self-view?

_____

_____

_____

_____

_____

False Assumptions

Gretchen grew up believing that her aunt, who always appeared well dressed, avoided visiting the family because their home was unkempt. This assumption led Gretchen to view herself and her family as sloppy folks who embarrassed the relatives. As an adult, Gretchen discovered evidence that her assumption was false. First, she heard relatives describe the aunt as "not the visiting type." Second, Gretchen visited her aunt on a vacation and was surprised to find the rooms very cluttered. It turns out her aunt was a fussy dresser, but not a fussy housekeeper. Gretchen had adopted an unnecessary humiliating view of herself as sloppy based on a false assumption. What influence have your false assumptions had on your self-view?

_____

_____

_____

_____

_____

Ongoing Influences

Even though you have a self-view that probably feels permanent, you *can* adjust it when you accept new information that proves it's wrong. In the previous example, Gretchen received new information and had to decide what to do with it. If she accepted it as the truth, she could then alter her self-view as a sloppy person posing as a neat person. If she chose to reject the news, her self-view would remain unchanged, reinforcing her false belief. This is one kind of ongoing influence.

Another type of influence could be called "current relationships." William Swann Jr., in his book *Self-Traps: The Elusive Quest for Higher Self-Esteem*, points out that once we are adults, external forces play an important role in forming our adult self-view. This is perhaps as important as analyzing our childhood influences. He suggests people must "scrutinize the relationships that sustain our conceptions of who we are." So, your ongoing influences may be a new truth (such as Gretchen's new discovery), as well as current relationships with family, friends, lovers, or co-workers, and fellow members of classes and churches. What are some of the ongoing influences creating your self-view?

_____

_____

_____

_____

_____

Your Personal Spin

The spin you put on (or, how you interpret) what has been done and said to you also influences your self-view. Your "personal spin" includes factors such as your temperament, experience, worldview, and concluding lens. In the preface of his book *A Question of Values,* Hunter Lewis quotes M. Scott Peck as saying that concluding lenses are the lenses through which we view ourselves and the world. The way we see the world results in different styles of thinking by which we make our value judgments and ethical decisions. When Mary, a client weary of being blocked by self-defeating behaviors, sorted through the origins of her self-view, she could see what is meant by "personal spin."

When Mary was seven, her parents moved her to a bedroom separated from the house by a breezeway. The distance from her parents' room frightened her. She became oversensitive to sounds at night and listened intently to news stories of burglaries. She created safety plans in her mind, hid a bat under her bed, and wouldn't play the radio for fear she would miss hearing the sound of an intruder turning the doorknob.

The spin Mary put on her parents' action was this: "The people I most trust will not protect me, therefore I am not worth protecting. My fears and safety don't matter to them, so I'm on my own if I want to be safe." Whether or not her conclusion was correct, it was based on real influencers. Her temperament was naturally compliant to authority, her parents were generally insensitive to the needs of a child, and their authoritative style left little or no room for Mary to express her fear.

Mary layered her conclusion about this incident upon other similar incidents and eventually they merged to become her proof that she didn't deserve good care by those close to her. She believed she must be worthless, or her parents—and others that followed—would have taken better care of her. Once this belief became her identity, she unconsciously set about to prove her opinion was correct. Seeing her friends sleeping in rooms close to their parents, for example, proved her belief that she didn't deserve the same level of care.

Other children, with different temperaments and sets of experiences, might have interpreted Mary's situation differently. Their conclusion may have been, "My parents trust me to sleep far away from them. I must be a very capable person."

We want to inform you about the persuasive power of two subtle "personal spins" that heavily influence your opinions about yourself. They are your temperament and your concluding lens.

Your Temperament

Your authentic, or inherent, responses are largely a result of your temperament. Discovering your temperament is a simple thing, and a wonderful one. The very act of discovering your temperament becomes a giant step in self-understanding, acceptance, and growth. We encourage you to identify your temperament with the following suggestions, if you don't already know what it is.

There are many personality and temperament assessment tools available today. One do-it-yourself assessment is the "Keirsey Temperament Sorter," created by David Keirsey. In the book *Please Understand Me* by David Kiersey and Marilyn Bates, they make the temperament sorter available, along with descriptions of each temperament quality. Their book is based on the work of Myers and Briggs who developed the Myers-Briggs Type Indicator, or the MBTI.

According to the work done by these and other researchers, your response to people and life spring from the following sets of operational preferences, which are general ways you prefer to feel, act, and operate in the world.

- Introvert or Extrovert

- Sensor or Intuitive

- Thinker or Feeler

- Perceiver or Judger

The following brief descriptions of these preferences will give you an idea of the influential nature of each:

Introvert (I): You are especially energized by retreating into a project and/or a few close friends.

Extrovert (E): You are especially energized by being with people and become restless when alone.

Sensor (S): You are practical (sensory) and "believe it when you see it."

Intuitive (N): You believe it when you have a hunch it is right.

Thinker (T): Your mind, or logic, motivates you. You make decisions with your head.

Feeler (F): Your emotions motivate you. You make decisions with your heart.

Perceiver (P): You prefer keeping your options open.

Judger (J): You prefer closure.

Your particular combination of these preferences, one from each set, indicate your temperament. Your temperament affects your self-view. For example, people with the preference combination of ENFP will be highly influenced by their feelings and the feelings and behaviors of others toward them. They will be very interested in the "He said – She said" of life. INTJs, on the other hand, will be influenced by their thoughts and logic and those resources and people they respect.

Your Concluding Lens

Here is yet another personal spin you use to form opinions about yourself, and anything else, for that matter. It is what author and columnist Hunter Lewis calls your "concluding lens." Lewis claims you have a *preferred* method of reaching conclusions. He has divided the methods, or "lenses," into six categories. If an idea makes sense to your concluding lens, you are more likely to embrace it. It is rather like running things by a wise friend whose perspective you like. If the friend gives it the "okay," you're more inclined to buy into it. If the friend doesn't see it as such a good thing, you will probably pass.

It's important to identify and use your lens when making decisions. We want to point out three things:

1. You will feel the most confident about your decisions when you and your concluding lens agree.

2. Your concluding lens, as valuable as it is, can overinfluence you.

3. You will assure yourself the greatest success when you use most or all of the lenses in making choices.

The lenses and their preferences include:

1. **Emotion:** I want to *feel* that it is right.

2. **Logic:** I want to know it makes *sense*.

3. **Science:** I want it to be *provable*.

4. **Authority:** I want an *expert opinion*.

5. **Sense and experience:** I want to *see, touch, taste, smell* it.

6. **Intuition:** I want to know it in my *gut*.

Which concluding lens do you believe is your preferred style? One way to find out is to ask yourself what kind of confirmation you usually seek to feel good about a choice you have made. Is it a certain feeling, is it a word from someone you respect, is it a sense of knowing, is it proof from research or studies, is it the experience itself or confirmation of past experience, or is it that the decision is so logical? You will feel better about your choice to increase your sense of treasuredness and create better boundaries when it makes sense to your concluding lens.

Your Self-View, or Esteem

Whether your self-esteem is high or low, here's what you need to know to understand its influence in steering you to certain choices:

- The latest research indicates your self-esteem is a result of how competent and how lovable you sense you are.

- Once you conclude you are either competent and lovable, or incompetent and unlovable, you will make choices that prove your conclusions are right.

If you have high self-esteem, and someone gives you a poor evaluation, you will either dismiss it or, more frequently, accelerate your positive behavior to prove the evaluation is incorrect.

If you have low self-esteem and someone gives you more praise than you are comfortable with, you will increase your negative behaviors so they will believe the praise was unworthy. In fact, so strong is people's desire to be right in their own self-view, that, as William Swann Jr. says in his book *Self-Traps: The Elusive Quest for Higher Self-Esteem*, "the more positive events they (those with high esteem) experienced, the better their health. In contrast, for people with low self-esteem, the more positive events they experienced, the worse their health." When our environment does not match our self-view, we become upset. Do you see the vital importance of this information? People unconsciously construct their lives to fit their level of self-esteem. If you believe you are a treasure, you will fill your life with people, things, and activities that prove it. If you believe you are trash, you will do the same.

The fallout of this explains, for example, why the partners and friends of people often feel left behind as their loved ones improve their beliefs about themselves. When someone's esteem goes from low to high, it becomes difficult to return to a relationship or environment that doesn't support the new self-belief. So, in effect, people do get left behind.

You picked up your first sense of competence and lovability from your primary caregivers and the other influences we have named. Now, as an adult, you conclude how lovable you are by your current relationships. By the way, if you're a product of the "lovable and capable" self-esteem movement, you may have been helped to a higher esteem, but you may have also been hurt by it. Some teachers and parents have come to believe that honesty about a child's abilities lowers their esteem, so they overpraise and falsely commend them. Children know the truth, so when they receive false praise it often backfires and causes them to believe the adult really wants them to be someone they aren't. This only reinforces a sense of low competence and lovability.

What influence is your self-esteem having on your life?

———————————————————————————————

———————————————————————————————

———————————————————————————————

———————————————————————————————

———————————————————————————————

Respecting the Strength of Your Beliefs about Yourself

You are inclined to reject proof that your self-beliefs are wrong. In other words, dislodging them is something only an owner of a life can do. There is a story of a man who went to his psychiatrist and said, "I am dead." Nothing seemed to shake him from this delusion. The psychiatrist, in an attempt to jolt the man out of his false opinion, asked him to go home and look into the mirror each day for thirty days and say, "Dead men don't bleed." At the end of thirty days, the man returned to the psychiatrist, who was eagerly anticipating a breakthrough. The moment came to test his theory. The psychiatrist took a pin and pricked the end of his patient's index finger. A drop of blood appeared on the surface of the finger and the psychiatrist asked, "Now what do you believe?" The patient replied, "Dead men do bleed." If you don't want your misbeliefs out of your life, no one can remove them for you.

Your beliefs about yourself are strong. They have taken root and like living with you. By shifting to a new opinion, or adopting a new personal identity about your value, you are essentially trading in outdated opinions for new ones. This is a lot to ask of both your unconscious and conscious self. It is like interrupting a basketball game and changing the rules. The players would say, "We only play by these rules," the fans would say, "We're outta here," and the referees would cry, "You can't do this!" Shifting to treasuredness and effective boundaries can be just as dramatic—and interesting!

The strength of false opinions can be broken through gradual, intentional shifts, or through sudden, jolting ones that catch us off guard, as described in the story of Maya Angelou at the beginning of this section. Her strong opinion of herself was that she was too worthless to own beautiful things. Out of that opinion, a piece of her identity was formed. She unconsciously identified herself as a black woman who could not own beautiful things, which resulted in conscious decisions limiting the quality or beauty of things she could own. Her opinion was created from real comments, societal beliefs, impressions, and experiences, yet her opinion was incorrect. Since this part of her identity was built on a false belief, it too was false.

The beautiful furnishings Maya Angelou's husband bought for her didn't fit into her identity, so her first reaction was to reject the gift. This jolt helped her look at the situation again and see the truth. She came to understand that her identity as a woman who could not own beautiful things was based on her opinion that she was worthless. By rejecting this racist and sexist opinion, she was able to adjust her identity and come to a new conclusion: "I am a worthwhile black woman who can, indeed, own beautiful things."

You commonly reject what doesn't fit your identity. If you believe you are unlovable, you will reject love. If you believe you are dumb, you will reject the possibility you are intelligent. If you believe you are boring, you will reject being described as interesting. Your opinions of yourself greatly determine your identity, and your identity usually determines what you will and won't let into your life—good or bad. So, if you hold an opinion that you are less valuable than others, you will adopt an identity that matches your opinion, and you will reject evidence that you are wrong. You will set limits, or boundaries, that keep you comfortable in your delusion *until* you choose not to anymore.

As strong as false beliefs about yourself are, they are not more powerful than your decision to change. You are the owner of your life and you can "clean house" on self-fulfilling prophecies that imprison you. Ruth, an entrepreneur in her thirties, did just that. Prior to owning her own business, Ruth was criticized by a co-worker for being aloof and hard to approach. The co-worker's comment closed with, "And everyone knows it."

Ruth felt she went out of her way to make people feel comfortable, yet she had noticed that co-workers were sometimes less inclined to relax with her than with others. After the co-worker's comment, what started as a tentative belief Ruth had about herself being unfriendly began to take full root. Her confidence in meeting with staff dwindled. Her belief began to prove itself in her behavior. When meeting people, Ruth assumed they would find her unapproachable and therefore unlikable. This was a lie. Ruth was well liked by most of the staff and she had many close and lasting friendships. Over time Ruth recognized her distorted belief was a lie and one day she was finally able to toss it aside. She would then consciously change the belief, and replace it with a more accurate belief, "I can sometimes appear aloof and unapproachable because of my intensity, but I am good at dispelling that perception with friendliness."

At times in the years following the eviction of the "aloof lie," Ruth would be tempted to readopt it. When she would find herself withdrawing, or assuming people she met were having negative thoughts about her, she would reject the old lie. Ruth would then intentionally extend herself to the other person with sincerity.

The interesting thing about our opinions of ourselves is that we can live a lifetime and not know they are inaccurate. What we will know is that life seems out of sync somehow, like it never really comes together in a satisfying way. In fact, life is out of sync when our negative self-view interferes with what is really true. The opinion you have of yourself will show in your personality and in the types of boundaries you set.

Your Beliefs Determine Your Boundaries

What you believe about yourself will determine what boundaries you set. As you adjust your beliefs so that you own your life and become your own best friend, your boundaries will shift naturally to match your beliefs. Your core beliefs about yourself produce certain perceptions, and, in turn, those perceptions produce certain behaviors. When it comes to setting a boundary, say, between your parents' negative opinion of living in a big city and your desire to live the urban life, this choice will spring from your beliefs about your power to make a choice that may go against your parents' wishes. If your belief is that you enjoy but don't need the approval of your parents to make a decision, your perception will be that you are free to make your own choices, and you will move to the city. If your belief is that you must maintain the approval of your parents even when it goes against your own desires, then your perception is that you are powerless against their wishes, and you will not move to the city. In either case, your choice of boundaries would have reflected your beliefs and the perceptions that spring from those beliefs.

Like the other influences we have presented to you, your core beliefs can cause you to perceive things differently than someone else might. Dr. Rian McMullin puts it this way in his book *Handbook of Cognitive Therapy Techniques,* "A harsh word from a spouse prompts different reactions in two different people, primarily because of their differing underlying belief structures, which color how they perceive the criticism. The person who is firmly convinced of his or her personal inferiority accepts the criticism as another confirmation of the validity of that belief, and might experience severe emotional discomforts in this and other aspects of life. The person who is confident may see the criticism as a reflection of the spouse's unhappiness and frustration."

It is important to know your core beliefs to understand your perceptions, and therefore your choices and reactions to the people and circumstances in your life. Distorted core beliefs will result in distorted boundaries, a sure ticket to either a chaotic or boring life. Remember, your beliefs are your reality, even if they are false, and you will struggle to prove them right—even if they are wrong—so you can live in a way you're used to and comfortable with. Change sometimes can seem more frightening than the current unhappiness, simply because you don't know what to expect.

Your job as owner of your life is to identify and adjust your misbeliefs. We will help you through this process in later chapters. This will immediately affect your boundaries. It is a great moment when you realize you have shifted to a new, better place of thinking. You might be at a dance, for example, and hear yourself say "no, thanks," to an unpleasant person you would have said "yes" to just last weekend. As you refuse the invitation, you surprise yourself and experience a rush of personal freedom. The world didn't crumble, the music didn't stop, and the crowd didn't point to you and call you names. Your new boundary grew directly out of a shift in your core belief. You adjusted your belief to be, "I can choose to let only people I enjoy get physically close to me."

Reminding Yourself

- Your opinions and beliefs about yourself are a compilation of various life influences, including your personal spin, temperament, and concluding style.

- Self-esteem is determined by how competent and lovable you sense you are.

- Once you adopt an opinion—negative or positive—about yourself, you arrange your life to prove your opinion is right.

- Your core beliefs create perceptions that determine your actions.

- As owner of your life, you are the only one who can adjust your beliefs, treasure yourself, and create effective boundaries.

- People choose to create new boundaries for themselves every day!

8

Identifying False Beliefs

Let's begin the hunt for the knowledge you seek so you can be well equipped to make the adjustments you desire. In this chapter, we inform you about the symptoms of misbeliefs, outline the common types of internal resistors, show you how to identify and draw lines against them, and present an assortment of change strategies.

At age forty-five, Angela, began to adjust her beliefs about her value and set new boundaries to match. She had been attending an empowerment group to learn to speak up for herself. This was especially important because Angela was a victim of verbal abuse by her husband. She had lost her "voice" and was unable to speak her mind. Her core beliefs were that she was inferior to others, that she had less important things to say, that her feelings were insignificant, and that it wasn't worth the trouble it would cause if she did speak up. Angela's opinion statement might have read something like, "In my opinion, I am cooperative, nice, undeserving, powerless, overlooked, and mute. At times I feel worthless, too."

Angela's empowerment group had been studying a creative problem-solving model that taught them how to move from awareness to action—it taught them how to implement the boundaries they felt they needed. She attended the group for weeks before she gained the courage to try out the concept on her own.

Contemplating your action before actually making a move is quite typical.

Angela's new boundaries appeared for the first time the day she entered the grocery store and was treated badly by a clerk. The clerk accused Angela of giving him too little money and would not believe her when she denied it. Her new belief in her rights helped her to set boundaries and not let herself be taken advantage of. She now had the courage to apply the problem-solving model to the situation. Angela was aware that she was being mistreated. In her mind, she scanned her options and then made a choice: "Please call the manager." This was a giant step for a woman who had never in her memory stood up for herself. The clerk, seeing trouble ahead if the manager was called, quickly backpedaled and apologized. Angela left the store amazed. She had drawn a line and it had been respected. This action strengthened her new belief and equipped her to begin speaking her mind to others and, finally, to her husband. Fortunately, he was willing to make his own changes and they were able to continue their relationship, with new boundaries.

What caused Angela to believe she could not speak up for herself? Somewhere along the line, at home, or in school, she adopted the belief that her voice and opinions were insignificant, leading her to the perception that she didn't have a right to speak up when threatened. Based on her experiences, she placed her beliefs in an "internal folder" marked "Keep your mouth shut." Then, as opportunities to speak up came to her, her mind went to the cabinet, pulled out the file marked "Keep your mouth shut," and she did.

Through the empowerment group, a new way of thinking challenged the truth of her "Keep your mouth shut" file. She added a file called "Speak up if you want to." Now, when the time comes to voice an opinion or a need, and now that she has become aware of these files, Angela has a choice about which file to use. She has claimed ownership of her voice and is drawing new boundaries to preserve, protect, and present it.

Like Angela, you have a cabinet of internal files, or beliefs, that censor first your perceptions, then your actions. We all do. In order to change our behavior, we must become aware of our beliefs and perceptions, then assert ownership and make adjustments.

This chapter is filled with exciting information that will show you belief adjustment strategies from which you can create your own path of change. The first step in almost every change strategy is awareness, because until you realize something's not right, you can't fix it.

Becoming Aware

The fact that you are reading this book is a sign that you are already in the awareness stage. For one reason or another, you have become aware that your life needs better boundaries, or a deeper sense of ownership, or a higher level of personal treasuredness, or all three. Your awareness is the first step toward getting to the new behaviors you desire.

Awareness comes in many packages. Sometimes it's a general weariness of a constant internal struggle that keeps you tired and low. Other times life stops working, or working well enough, and a jolt of truth hits and can no longer be denied. And sometimes, something happens to force a person to reevaluate what they believe about themselves, which produces new behaviors. What has triggered your awareness?

Awareness can be a gift your life gives you that motivates you to want change more than you want to stay the same. It's actually quite a huge gift because as you now know, your beliefs resent change and, in fact, as William Swann Jr. describes in *Self-Traps: The Elusive Quest for Higher Self-Esteem*, "once people have incorporated a characteristic into their self-definition, they will have difficulty relinquishing that characteristic, *even if it brings them intense psychological or physical pain.* The key seems to be that firmly held self-views provide people with a sense of personal coherence that they value even more than they value positive changes."

Don't let the fierce hold of your false beliefs discourage you. Remember, you are the boss and your beliefs must answer to you. You can make changes starting right now. In fact, you have probably already started making them. Now we will move to the second important ingredient in changing your beliefs: knowledge.

Acquiring Knowledge

Once awareness hits, knowledge can step in and be heard. The more you know, the better off you are. The old cliché "Ignorance is bliss" is, well, ignorant because ignorance does not lead to knowledgeable solutions.

Acquiring knowledge today isn't difficult. It's everywhere, so be selective and *do not* seek knowledge from anyone whose life you don't admire; anyone who is a pessimist, a gossip, a controller, or a poor listener; anyone who has contributed to your false beliefs; anyone who uses people rather than respects them; or anyone who puts you down or makes you feel put down. This is setting boundaries, and we ask you to set them so that you can protect and preserve your move to new beliefs. Our first stop along the knowledge path is to look at the symptoms faulty beliefs produce.

Recognizing the Symptoms of Your False Beliefs

When something is out of alignment, things connected to it don't work. If it's your back, your movement can become limited. If it's your tires, your steering can become erratic. If it's your life, you can lose sight of your true purpose mission.

The following list of symptoms will help you determine if your life is out of alignment due to false beliefs. Most people's lives are out of alignment in some way, that is why ongoing, intentional change is vital to a happy, fulfilled life. Otherwise, people get tangled in the arms of yesterday and miss the wonder of today and tomorrow. These are symptoms, in general, of beliefs that are working against you:

1. Strong feeling states, out of proportion to the situation

2. Strong reactions, also out of proportion to the situation

3. Repetition of the same mistakes, problems, or losses

4. Marginal, listless, lackluster living

5. A life that feels out of sync

6. Roadblocked relationships, careers, certain emotions, and personal growth

7. Internal conflict between who and what you know you are, as opposed to how your life is being lived

8. Inordinate amount of excuse-making, shame, guilt, sadness, depression

9. Abuse in any form to you or from you

10. Self-views that do not match the evaluations of others about you

11. Active addictions, compulsions, and aversions to behaviors (such as sex, lying, gossip, pleasing, masturbation, exercise, or bulimia/anorexia) and substances (food, drugs, alcohol, cigarettes).

Do you recognize any of these symptoms in your life? The list is not exhaustive, but it does get the point across: If your life isn't in a *pattern* of thriving, something is amiss. Something is resisting your movement toward wholeness and happiness. These internal resistors need to be exposed, and in some cases evicted, from your life. To help you make that happen, we will now familiarize you with common internal resistors.

Identifying Common Internal Resistors

You face boundary violators in one form or another every day, from both inside and outside yourself. The boundary threats outside yourself are fairly easy to recognize: salespeople at your door or on your phone demanding your time, your kids asking you to spend more money than you've set aside, a spouse wanting you to loan money to an unreliable relative, and your boss putting subtle pressure on you to work overtime.

The boundary violators from within yourself can be trickier to spot, yet they can be equally harmful. As Buddha said, "Your worst enemy cannot harm you as much as your own thoughts, unguarded." If you are to be your own best friend, treasure yourself as if you were the ruby slippers, and if you are going to protect, preserve, and present yourself most effectively, you will want to become skilled at recognizing, withstanding, and overpowering your internal boundary violators, or resistors.

We refer to these internal boundary violators as "resistors" because they resist you making changes for your own good. Just as an electronic resistor blocks vital energy to the waiting receiver, an internal resistor wants to block positive transformations from you. If it sounds serious, it is. You want Life; but internal resistors (which have been set up as defense mechanisms, as we discuss later) are blocking you from the full expression of it.

Your Internal Resistors

The most common sources of internal resistors can be divided into four categories:

Ignorance

You can bumble through plenty of things and still come through somewhat competent, but do you really want to bumble through life? Ignorance is no match for knowledge. Knowledge is your path to clearing up many misconceptions and false beliefs. Once you know what they are, you are equipped to do or believe things differently. Just think of the times when once you were provided with new information, you thought, "Oh, I didn't know." You then looked at the person or situation in a completely new way. Ignorance can be damaging; and it can also keep you from knowing what you need to know to love yourself and set boundaries that honor you. We urge you to launch a personal campaign against your own ignorance as a frontline defense against internal resistors.

Misbeliefs

Misbeliefs, interchangeably used with false beliefs, are inaccuracies you adopt about yourself, life, and the world. Misbeliefs may be as harmless as believing if you work hard enough you can become anything you want, to more dangerous beliefs like if you were only a more loving wife your husband wouldn't hit you. Misbeliefs will keep you from building your life on the truth and sometimes they develop a pattern called "thinking errors."

Thinking Errors

A thinking error is a misbelief that has grown into a pattern of distorted thinking, producing inappropriate and exaggerated responses to life and circumstances. Thinking errors are serious threats to the person who wants to thrive; however, they're not uncommon and we all experience them from time to time. The duration of a thinking error may be short or sustained, depending on how aware and determined you are to build your life on truth. Thinking errors will cause you to respond in predictable and illogical ways. Therefore, we can't stress enough the importance of working toward exposing and removing these powerful resistors.

There are dozens of thinking errors; however, Dr. David Burns in the *New Mood Therapy*, simplified things considerably by identifying ten of the most common "cognitive distortions," or thinking errors. As you study the list, note any patterns that ring true for you.

1. **All-or-nothing thinking:** You look at things in absolute, black-and-white terms. "I gave in to my husband's unreasonable demands this morning, so now I've blown my chance to change that pattern."

2. **Overgeneralization:** You view a single negative event as a never-ending pattern of defeat. "This always happens to me."

3. **Mental filter:** You dwell on one negative detail, so your vision of the entire situation becomes dark and cloudy, like the drop of ink that discolors the entire beaker of water. "I know my performance was terrible because the boss suggested afterward that I need to make better eye contact with the client."

4. **Discounting the positive:** You insist that your positive qualities or accomplishments don't count. "Yeah, well, I'm nothing compared to Maxine."

5. **Jumping to conclusions:**

   - Mind reading—you assume people are reacting negatively to you when there is no definite evidence for this. "He obviously felt uncomfortable with my comments."

   - Fortune-telling—you arbitrarily predict that things can't change or will turn out badly. "We'll never see her again."

6. **Magnifying or minimizing:** You blow things out of proportion or shrink their importance inappropriately. "I guess you could say my dad beat me when I was a kid, but I deserved it."

7. **Emotional reasoning:** You reason from how you feel. "I feel like a failure, therefore I must really be one."

8. **"Should" statements:** You criticize yourself or other people with "should" or "shouldn't." "I should have known," "I shouldn't have missed his point." These are cousins to "ought," "have to," and "must."

9. **Labeling:** You identify with your shortcomings and mistakes and label yourself as a "fool" or "jerk" instead of pinpointing the cause of the problem so you can learn from it or try to correct it. "She's upset with me again. I'm such a jerk."

10. **Personalization and blame:** You blame yourself for something you weren't entirely responsible for (such as becoming ill or getting a divorce). Conversely, you may blame other people, external events, or fate, and overlook the ways your own attitudes and behavior have contributed to the problem. "I shouldn't have gone to the basketball game; my son never plays well when I'm there."

Defense Mechanisms

You, and every other person, have a defense system you have built over time to relieve tension and shield yourself from painful experiences. Your defense system contains both mature and immature defense mechanisms. As children, immature defense mechanisms were all we had. As adults, we can choose to replace them with mature defenses.

It can be argued that whatever is causing you emotional upset today exists because at earlier times in your life, times when life seemed too difficult to deal with, you cut the pain off in order to survive it. You may have tried to run from it, block it, eat, drink, or drug it away, or you may have slept to get the desired relief. These defensive walls, built to keep you safe from harm and danger, now trap you within your own prison. These immature defense mechanisms are unconscious, knee-jerk responses to pain and discomfort and aren't in your best interest or the interest of others. They are a troublesome assortment of escape maneuvers to cut off pain, pretend it isn't there, deflect it, discount it, or in some other way avoid it. Immature defense mechanisms keep you from confidently facing life.

Now that you are an adult, you can acquire desirable mature defense mechanisms. They are intentional and conscious responses to pain and discomfort and are in your best interest and the interest of others. They free you to face life confidently.

To demonstrate a mature and an immature defense mechanism in the same situation, let's say a conflict arises between you and your spouse in a store. If you implement a mature defense mechanism, you might acknowledge the conflict and then postpone resolving it until you are at home and calm. If, on the other hand, you use an immature defense mechanism, you might stuff your feelings and deny the conflict or blurt out angry, blaming words there in the aisle.

Because immature defense mechanisms operate on the unconscious level, they will keep you in the same pattern of disappointments, frustrations, and sadness until you're shocked or escorted into awareness by life events or people, or until you go on a hunt to uncover them and remove them from your life.

In order to recognize your defense system, it's important for you to become somewhat familiar with the most common immature and mature defense mechanisms. Dr. Robert Waldinger has identified the following explanations of defense mechanisms in his book, *Psychiatry for Medical Students*.

Immature Defense Mechanisms

Repression: This is the most basic mechanism of defense and underlies all others. When you repress, you seem to forget and force thought, memories, and feelings out of awareness. For example, the typical response of repression is "I don't remember."

Denial: You unconsciously distort or disbelieve reality in order to avoid pain. You might say, "If I don't acknowledge the growing lump in my breast, it isn't really there."

Retroflexion: You unconsciously turn against yourself by taking the blame for an angry outburst by another person. You might say, "I probably deserved to be yelled at in the meeting by my secretary because I could have been more sensitive to her mood."

Hypochondriasis: You shift your anger or resentment into physical complaints. You might, for example, be upset by the disrespectful behavior you are receiving from your child and transform your anger into tension headaches.

Acting out: You act on an unconscious desire in order to avoid being aware of the emotion that goes with it. For example, you have a sexual longing for a co-worker and act it out by engaging in promiscuous sex with others.

Projection: You reject your own motives and feelings that aren't okay to you and unconsciously attribute them to others instead. For example, you're feeling angry about your own issues at work but instead of facing them you accuse your wife of being angry when she isn't angry at all.

Splitting: You shift into compartmentalized thinking about yourself and others, seeing yourself and the world as all good or all bad. For example, you are upset by someone you have cared for and that you perceived as "all good," so you transfer them in your mind to "all bad" and end the relationship.

Reaction formation: Your unconscious impulses that aren't okay to you are dismissed and replaced with opposite conscious attitudes and behaviors. For example, a man whose strong sexual urges are severely repressed may react by leading a campaign for censorship of lewd and obscene literature in school libraries.

Intellectualization: You make strong emotions okay by thinking about them in neutral terms rather than experiencing them fully. For example, your husband lost his job and neutralizes and dismisses his fear by saying "I never wanted to work there anyway."

Isolation of affect: You isolate, or separate, your feelings from your thoughts in your memory. For example, a doctor may become callous and isolated from the pain of his patients.

Mature Defense Mechanisms

Altruism: You give constructive, satisfying service to others, including philanthropy.

Humor: You're able to express your feelings and deal with uncomfortable thoughts and situations without causing distress to yourself or others.

Suppression: You consciously decide to postpone dealing with a painful situation until a more appropriate time.

Anticipation: You plan ahead for future discomfort, such as the death of a parent.

Sublimation: You deny animalistic impulses that are not socially acceptable.

Other Common Internal Resistors

The following internal resistors don't fall on a particular list, but they can be tormenting and will often block you from growth:

Shame: Distorts your sense of personal worth as a human being who is both good and bad.

False guilt: Distorts your belief about what you are and aren't.

Entitlement: Distorts the way you think about what you deserve.

Scapegoating: Distorts personal responsibility.

Thinking errors and defense mechanisms show up in most of our lives to varying degrees. It's when they become a pervasive *pattern* that they become a problem. Thinking errors and defense mechanisms can serve as temporary protective boundaries between you and painful or uncontrollable experiences. They help you keep your balance until you can face what has happened: until you can manage your difficult realities. The trouble comes when the defenses you created under dire circumstances are no longer needed, but you still use them. Ironically, the defenses you used to defend and protect yourself from pain as a child become unconscious shackles that chain you to a defensive bunker as an adult. It is as if you're hiding behind your defenses in fear of pain instead of moving beyond them and risking life as an intentional adult.

Sara is an example of how denial can imprison a person. She came to see us following the breakup of what she described as a "very positive" long-term relationship. She reported that this was actually the second time a positive relationship was terminated by a man in her life because she "couldn't commit." Sara was confused and frustrated. "Why do I do this to myself? I know I could have been very happy with either one of the men I said good-bye to."

At first, Sara was unable to access the unconscious files that triggered her fear of commitment. After a time of focused attention on examining her belief system, Sara was able to see that her fear stemmed from her belief that "marriage kills relationships." This self-defeating belief stemmed from the following childhood experience: When Sara was six, her parents, who had not been married, decided to get married and have a big celebration. Within four months, however, her parents separated and not long after that, divorced. As a child, Sara was crushed, but as an adult she discounted and denied that this event was any big deal. Sara was in a pattern of denial; she was minimizing the impact of the event on her life.

Accepting Your Internal Resistors

"My resistors are not me." These encouraging words can make it easier to accept internal resistance as something that has attached itself to you. It actually stifles your true desires and identity and prevents you from making positive changes. Everyone alive, including you, has been influenced by ignorance, misbeliefs, thinking errors, and defense mechanisms. Once you accept the truth that internal resistors have negatively affected your life, you can get on with the work of breaking them down and letting them go.

Holding on to Thinking
Errors and Distortions

What is the price for holding on to your resistors? It's high—higher than it's worth. While ignoring thinking errors allows you to continue on a path that is familiar, it is a path laden with losses. Cal's life is an example of this. Cal is forty, attractive, married, smart, and an attentive father. While he has the intelligence and drive to succeed in his career, it has been filled with disappointing starts and stops. Why? Cal believes he is a powerful manager and leader, but people do not follow him for long. While he initially appears to be a leader, he soon becomes exhausting to those working with him. He is patronizing, a poor listener, has difficulty acknowledging what he doesn't know, and discounts the help competent people give him. When a project works, he takes the credit. When it doesn't, he casts blame. His life is being sabotaged by internal resistors and he is living out the frustrating losses they produce. He is in denial, has a pattern of both minimization and grandiosity, and is motivated by an underlying sense of inferiority, none of which he has yet acknowledged. Therefore, he remains semieffective when, in fact, if he would let go of his resistors, he could very well soar in his career and be the leader he believes himself to be.

Like Cal, to one degree or another, holding on to internal resistors will require you to give up:

- Personal freedom based on truth

- Personal responsibility

- Adventurous living

- Seeing the value and beauty in everyday experiences

- Dignity

- Agility in facing and solving problems

- Full expression of your authentic self

- Grace toward yourself and others

- Deep happiness and meaning

- Accurate perspective

- A sense of wholeness

Reminding Yourself

- There is no shame in discovering you have adopted false beliefs, thinking errors, and immature defenses.

- Awareness is the first step in adjusting your beliefs about yourself.

- Distorted thinking is like an internal resistor, blocking you from receiving Life.

- Every person experiences distorted thinking.

- The most common internal resistors are: ignorance, misbeliefs, thinking errors, and immature defense mechanisms.

- Symptoms of internal resistors show up in your life.

- Temporary misbeliefs and defense mechanisms may or may not develop into long-term patterns.

- It is important to acknowledge the presence of internal resistors in your life so you can adjust or remove them.

9

Adjusting the
Way You Think

You will adjust the way you think about yourself, life, and others in one of two ways: (1) you will identify the distorted belief causing the defeating behavior and change it, or, (2) you will change the behavior, letting it lead to a change in your beliefs. Most personal growth is a combination of these. You will naturally formulate your own program of change using your experience, the information we provide you, and the knowledge you gain from other sources.

Adjusting the way you think and overcoming your internal resistors is a courageous path made up of small steps and big rewards. We were pleased to read of one well-documented study of this step-by-step process in Dr. Stanton E. Samenow's book *Inside the Criminal Mind*. It relates how a Dr. Yochelson helped prisoners adjust their thinking in simple day-to-day ways. If everyone who had a thinking error was imprisoned, we'd all be in jail, so we've chosen this story not because it's a crime to have faulty thinking but because it's an inside look at the process in an environment that was measurable.

Dr. Samenow explains that Dr. Yochelson taught the criminals to become aware of and write down their day-to-day thinking without editing it in a self-serving manner. Daily, in small groups, the criminals reported that thinking and Yochelson identified the thinking errors and taught them the corrections. He also instructed them in how to deter the massive amounts of criminal thinking that occurred daily.

> As the men saw themselves realistically, they became fed up with their old ways and made efforts to change. Their progress was not rapid or smooth, for even though they did not want to return to crime, they did not find living responsibly particularly appealing either—at least not for awhile. The criminals had been accustomed to instant results in whatever they undertook, and these were not forthcoming. As they developed new patterns of thought and behavior, they slowly found that there were rewards, tangible and intangible. They did not have to look over their shoulders for the police, and they felt "clean." The criminals discovered that effort, competence, and reliability are usually rewarded and that they could accomplish worthwhile things without deception or intimidation. Responsible people, especially members of their families, began to trust them and react to them differently. The men were promoted in their jobs and began to acquire material possessions honestly. Gradually, criminal patterns were abandoned, and they acquired a new set of values by which they could live responsibly.

Swapping lies for truth requires change, and most people resist change until they understand that change is their stepping stone to improved living. One thing we want you to hear loud and clear: **Give yourself a break.** By choosing to improve your friendship with yourself and set better boundaries, you are tackling a major life-changing project. So, treat yourself gently while you do it, like a best friend would. Be honest, firm, and kind. There is no growth without change, and while it may not always be quick and easy, it is essential. The important thing is that you change what is blocking you from being your own best friend, owning your life, and setting better boundaries. There are many models and approaches for change available today. Allen Ivey, author of *Developmental Therapy*, writes, "Each therapeutic school, be it person-centered, cognitive-behavioral, or psychodynamic, has unique approaches that confront varying types of client discrepancies (or problems). Each of these methods, in addition, has its own conceptions of developmental growth and change. However, it may be argued that underlying the varying conceptions of change are methodological consistencies that may be identified and taught within a larger metatheoretical developmental frame." He goes on to list four ingredients essential to growth and transformation.

1. Knowledge of the change process itself

2. Structuring the environment for change

3. Use of developmentally appropriate interventions and theories to produce change

4. The prevention of relapse or loss of insight for change

These four essentials, in one form or another, are embedded in the strategies summarized for you in this chapter. Fortunately, you're living at a time when the science of change is producing valuable information to increase the success of positive, long-term results. The first work we will summarize is that of noted researcher Dr. James Prochaska in his helpful book, *Changing for Good*, which he coauthored with Drs. John C. Norcross and Carlo Diclemente.

The Process of Change

To determine how change most naturally happens, Dr. Prochaska and his colleagues studied self-changers—people who figured out on their own how to change their lifestyles in some way. The researchers not only identified the stages of change, but what strategies worked best in each stage. As you're preparing to change the way you think, this information will be helpful to you.

Before examining the stages and strategies, we want to pass along some particularly significant information contained in Dr. Prochaska's conclusions.

- The key to successful change is to apply strategies that fit a particular stage.

- The stages of change remain the same no matter what a person is trying to change.

- Any increased knowledge about yourself or your area of needed change will increase your chance of lasting success.

- Failure to change usually increases your chance to succeed the next time.

- Change cannot be forced, yet it is possible to set the process of change in motion before you are ready to act.

- Your chances of lasting change increase when you give yourself two or more alternatives to the behavior you are changing.

- It is vital that you know what stage of change you are in at any given time so you can apply its most effective strategies.

- You need different types of help from people at each stage.

Dr. Prochaska and his colleagues have identified six stages of change that every self-changer cycles through. They are

1. **Precontemplation:** I am not interested in changing and I am not certain I even have a problem.

2. **Contemplation:** I am aware I have a problem and am entertaining the idea of change.

3. **Preparation:** I have decided to change and am preparing to take action.

4. **Action:** I am taking action to overcome my problem behavior.

5. **Maintenance:** I am maintaining change through the use of various change strategies.

6. **Termination:** This issue is no longer a problem for me.

Since you're reading this book, it's safe to assume you're either in the contemplation or preparation stage of changing your personal boundary system. In this stage, you are open to new information and to the possibility of changing the way you treat yourself and let others treat you.

In personal growth and boundary work, you move from change to change in an upward spiral. One of the biggest challenges in setting and maintaining boundaries is that by their very nature, boundaries are in flux, because situations and people change. What once was a big deal is no longer reason for an inflexible boundary; what used to be trivial has now become critical. The line you drew between you and your old drinking buddy can be erased because he or she is sober now, too.

The process of change, then, is an integral element to treasuring yourself, owning your life, and setting boundaries. Growth requires change. Change has a path. If you want to get good at being your own best friend, you want to get good at the process of change and at tolerating being in different stages with different issues. For example, you may be in the action stage when it comes to believing you are a talented fund-raiser, but in the precontemplation stage in believing you are capable of a long-term relationship. Similarly, you may be in the contemplation stage about setting boundaries with an overattentive friend and in the maintenance stage about not bringing work home.

Precontemplation Stage Strategies

Remember, in this stage you are resistant.

- Raise your consciousness through knowledge.

- Become aware of your defenses.

- Note social support for the change you're seeking to make: support groups, counselors, books, and workplace seminars.

- Give these instructions to your change helper(s): Don't push me into action. I'm not ready. I'm trying to be more open and less defensive, talk to me, give me feedback, don't give up, don't enable me, let me feel your care. Period.

Contemplation Stage Strategies

Remember, in this stage you are warming up to the idea of change.

- Continue raising your consciousness through knowledge and awareness: pay attention, notice your defenses, read, observe, inquire, and listen.

- Emotionally arouse yourself: watch movies where the characters deal with your issue; use your imagination to create negative scenes about your problem in your mind (limit negative scenes to the precontemplation and contemplation stages).

- Complete self-reevaluations: take stock, ask yourself serious questions like, "Knowing what I now know, can I truly respect myself if I continue this behavior?

- Give these instructions to your change helper(s): Please be empathetic, genuinely caring, and warm. Like me no matter how well I do, give me information and knowledge in noncondemning or controlling ways, and remember I am in charge of my own change.

Preparation Stage Strategies

Remember, in this stage you are preparing to change.

- Continue self-reevaluations.

- Commit to the change: Your commitment means you have a willingness to act and to believe in your ability to change. It is "an act of faith" in yourself.

- Reduce the anxiety of change by taking small steps.

- Set a date to begin.

- "Go public" by telling someone you are committing to making a change.

- Create your own plan of action.

- Give these instructions to your change helper(s): I want your help, but please don't keep asking how I am doing. Don't nag me. Offer to help when I look overwhelmed and tell me how proud you are that I am doing this.

Action Stage Strategies

Remember, in this stage you are taking action!

- Counter old behaviors by substituting healthy ones: refocus, exercise, relax, and apply counterthinking and assertiveness.

- Control your environment: change your surroundings and situations.

- Reward yourself: personal pats on the back, contracting with yourself or someone else for a reward when a particular goal is reached.

- Give yourself time for the process to work.

- Give these instructions to your change helper(s): Stick with me, do things with me, and help me get rid of the triggers. Encourage me and stay positive. Don't nag, preach, or embarrass me.

Maintenance Stage Strategies

Remember, in this stage you are maintaining the changes you have made.

- Continue using the change processes, including reviewing the difficulties you have both encountered and overcome in your process of change.

- Take credit for your accomplishments.

- In early maintenance, avoid triggers—people, places, and things that could jeopardize your change.

- Create a new lifestyle.

- Say and think positive things to yourself.

- Rate your belief in your success if you were to return to triggering situations.

- Give these instructions to your change helper(s): Don't forget what I've accomplished. Confront me if I start relapsing and remind me of the negative aspects of my problem if I ask you to.

How do these "Stages of Change" translate to the issues of treasuring yourself, owning your life, and setting boundaries? They will be as individual as you are, but the following is an example of one possibility:

Applying Stages of Change to Treasuring, Ownership, and Boundaries

Stage	Treasuredness	Ownership	Boundaries
Precontemplation "Not interested in change"	"Nothing but a bunch of fluff."	"All I need is one more thing to be responsible for."	"What is a boundary?"
Contemplation "Interested in changing"	"I guess being my own best friend does make sense."	"I would like to be more in charge of my life."	"You mean it's okay for me to set limits?"
Preparation "In pursuit"	"I want to learn about treasuring myself."	"I'm preparing to take back ownership of my life."	"I'm studying my existing boundaries to see where they are strong or weak."
Action "Doing it"	"I am actively making choices to treasure myself."	"I am taking responsibility for my thoughts, feelings, and behavior."	"I am adjusting my boundaries to let good in and keep bad out."
Maintenance "Continuing"	"I am continuing to grow in my friendliness toward myself."	"I am the owner of my life and am learning what that really means!"	"I continue to reexamine and adjust my boundaries."

Note: The termination stage does not apply to personal growth!

As you make decisions about being your own best friend and setting effective boundaries, you'll be making a choice to change. When you're ready for a more detailed look at proven change strategies, you may want to purchase a book such as Dr. Prochaska's. This is a friendly thing to do for yourself!

Adjusting Your Environment

Make some positive adjustments in your environment to increase the speed and effectiveness of learning to treasure yourself and set better boundaries. When your environment supports any effort at change, the success of that change is strengthened. You may ask, "How do I structure my environment for treasuring myself?" You replace what isn't treasuring to you with what is— this can include objects, relationships, words you speak, or simply what you wear. For example, Allie, who manages a hectic boutique in downtown Manhattan, adjusted her environment by choosing not to answer the phone after eight because that was her time to relax, read, listen to music, or think about her life. Mike, who was battling his low self-esteem issues, selected, framed, and displayed several relevant quotes throughout his home. Similarly, Leslie found that certain people brought her down and she gradually turned away from them and toward those who enhanced, rather than diminished her. As you begin to treasure yourself, you'll make adjustments in your environment naturally. In the meantime, there are some very positive and encouraging steps you can take to rouse the support of your surroundings, such as

- Remove items from your home, office, and closet you don't enjoy.

- Rearrange anything like schedules, furniture, accessories, or color schemes that don't seem to quite "fit" you anymore.

- Display treasured objects to remind yourself of your value, such as a rare coin, prized heirloom, or a photograph of a beloved relative.

- Develop deeper relationships with positive, supportive people.

- Learn something new, which is a secret of life that most miss.

- Place motivating books, CDs, and images at your finger-tips at home, in your office, and in your car so you can support your desire to be your own best friend at a moment's notice.

Intervention Strategies

The following intervention strategies can be useful tools for treasuring, owning, and protecting your life. Read through them to see which ones appeal to you.

The Stand-In Treasure Strategy

There are times when we cannot muster up a level of esteem that motivates us to make good choices for ourselves. Maybe we've just experienced a big disappointment, or we've somehow blown it, or we're feeling hopeless about making truly positive changes. If it were up to us, we would not treat ourselves well, and so, out of a place of self-disgust, we choose behaviors that are not in our best interest.

When you are in this situation, try this strategy—imagine that someone you treasure is in your place and make your choice as if you are making it for them.

For example, Harriet has taken a job that she has no passion for because she needs more money than her freelance design work was bringing in. Even though she knows it's short-term while her daughter Kris is in high school, she is discouraged and misses her "real" work as an artist. Her sagging esteem is tempting her to adopt old patterns of sabotage around food and exercise. She knows she is headed for weight gain and loss of energy, but doesn't want to go there. So, Harriet is learning to temporarily substitute her daughter as the treasured object and make her food and exercise choices as if she were making them for her daughter.

When Harriet is standing in front of the refrigerator choosing between nectarines or a bowl of ice cream at ten at night, she thinks, "What choice would I want Kris to make?" Because she values Kris and wants what's good for her, the choice is clear. "Because I treasure Kris and want the best for her, I would want her to choose the nectarines, therefore nectarines are the best choice for me, too." Harriet is using Kris as a "stand-in treasure" until she gets to a personal space that allows her to treasure herself.

The Stand-In Beliefs Strategy

A similar strategy to using a "stand-in treasure" is to use "stand-in beliefs." You may want to use this strategy when your beliefs about yourself in some area are not in line with what you know is true. The "stand-in beliefs" strategy works like this: until you can believe in yourself, your value, or your treasuredness, you will use the belief someone else has of you. Here are some examples.

- Patricia, an accomplished composer, used her professor's belief of her "intellectual brilliance" as a stand-in for her lack of belief in her left-brained intelligence.

- Charles used his father-in-law's belief in him as "compassionate" when he was being influenced by memories of a former friend calling him "selfish and uncaring."

- Hilary used her husband's belief in her as "lively and entertaining" as a stand-in when her thinking error influenced her to believe she was a boring and uninteresting woman.

- Diane used the beliefs her son wrote about her on a birthday card as a stand-in when her belief in her abilities as a mother weakened.

Use the positive beliefs others hold of you in the same way. If you can remember positive words and comments people you value have said about you, use them as stand-ins when your own self-beliefs need a boost. Other sources of stand-in beliefs include

- Favorable job evaluations

- Greeting cards and letters

- Inscriptions

- Performance reviews

- Testimonials

We have encountered some people who've never received a positive affirmation from another human being or, because their thinking error blocked them from "hearing" positive comments, they don't remember receiving any. Others are in a situation where they no longer receive encouragement and positive beliefs about themselves from their family and friends. If either of these circumstances are true for you, we urge you to

- Recall positive comments people have made to you, such as a co-worker's compliment about your ability to work with people, a friend's remark about your loyalty, or a child's description of you as "fun."

- Initiate contact with people who can affirm you, such as groups or clubs that focus on something you care about. A book club, for example, enables you to enrich your life through reading and discussion and opens up the chance for a relationship with someone who shares your interest.

- Practice giving yourself credit for acts of kindness, love, and responsibility. It's important for you to be doing what pleases you. While praise from others is valuable, inner appreciation, regardless of praise from others, is at least as important.

The Stepping-Over-Feelings Strategy

Sometimes your desire to act as your own best friend is blocked by your negative feelings. This is when you might choose to employ the following "stepping-over-feelings" strategy. This strategy is based on the mature defense mechanism of "postponement," meaning you acknowledge the feeling, knowing a misbelief may be causing it, then choose to postpone attention to the belief and its feeling until a later, more appropriate, time. You "step over the feeling" and do what you were hesitant to do anyway, saying, "I feel scared, nevertheless, I will move forward." Two of our personal experiences fit well here as an example of the "stepping-over-feelings" strategy.

Greg had flown from Oregon to New York to attend a creative problem-solving conference. During one of the sessions, the participants were led in a series of activities designed to express their creativity through movement, including a form of dance. Greg was feeling especially self-conscious about joining in on the activity since he hadn't danced for years. For just a moment, Greg stood on the sidelines contemplating opting out of the activity because of the tension he was experiencing between what he felt and what he believed.

Greg's belief was, "I want to fully participate in this event and get the most out of the growth experience." However, his feeling was, "I may make a fool of myself in front of these people I have come to know this week." If Greg were to make a choice as his own best friend, what choice would it be? Would he decide with his feelings to remain sidelined, or postpone his fear, and in turn live out his belief that personal growth, while at times uncomfortable, will be in his best interest?

Greg chose to be his own best friend by treating himself to the dance. He "stepped over his feelings" in this case and chose what he believed was a higher good. His choice proved to be a liberating moment that has motivated him to stretch in other areas of creative expression as well.

Jan experienced a similar breakthrough when she went on vacation with her husband and their grown children. She was very excited about the trip but knew she would be facing a big challenge at the pool. For years, Jan had managed to avoid being seen in public in a swimsuit. She had feelings of shame and self-consciousness about her plumpness. If Jan succumbed to these feelings, she would be a timid observer rather than a joyful participant. Jan is rather accomplished at talking herself through issues, but this one had dug its heels in and didn't want to let go. She wanted to make a choice that was in her own best interest and the interests of the family. Her feelings told her that her loving family would be horrified by her bare shape, that they would be embarrassed to be with her, and that onlookers should be spared such a sight. Her true beliefs conflicted with these feelings. She believed her family loved her regardless of her size or shape, and that even if people found her body unpleasant to look at it they really wouldn't care, and that being a grandmother having a truly wonderful time cannonballing into the pool with the kids overcomes flabby thighs and arms any day.

Jan's feelings were strong enough that she chose to acknowledge them to her family. So, when the moment came to go to the pool in street clothes or swimwear, Jan simply stated, "I want you to know that I am embarrassed to have you see me in a swimsuit because of my size and condition, but I am choosing to have fun at the pool anyway because I know you love me and care more about who I am than how I look." Her family wholeheartedly affirmed her belief. At some point during the week, she realized her feelings had been postponed, and she was playing in the water undistracted.

So, while it's important to pay attention to your feelings, there are times to step over them and act on the beliefs that are in your overall best interest. Then, when the time is right, deal with the feelings and the situations that caused your initial hesitation.

The Choose Your Emotion, Change Your Behavior Strategy

This strategy is an interesting spin on the "step-over-feelings" strategy. In their book *The Emotional Hostage*, Leslie Bandler-Cameron and Michael Lebeau present a plan for change that suggests you determine what feelings produce the behavior you want and then access those feelings to produce the behavior.

For example, if you wanted to be your own best friend by getting the most out of a conference you were attending, you would ask yourself what behaviors would be in your best interest. If you selected friendliness (for networking), attentiveness (to gather data), and confidence (in personal presentation), the authors suggest you identify and access what feelings make you friendly, attentive, and confident, so that you can authentically be those things. If this interests you, pick up their book to learn how to expand and utilize your emotions to adjust what you do to become your own best friend.

The Thought-Stopping Techniques Strategy

Here is a compilation of countering and behavioral techniques that can help you stop certain thoughts:

- Place a rubber band around your wrist; snap it when you are behaving *unlike* your own best friend.

- Imagine a STOP sign in your mind; let it stop you from untreasured behaviors and beliefs.

- Set boundaries against self-diminishing thoughts and actions. When you catch yourself in the throes of thinking errors, say, "No, I won't go there."

- Collect an assortment of written proofs of your competence and/or lovability and read them when you doubt it.

- When you do something that proves your competence and lovability, write it down and use it as proof against misbeliefs and negative feelings.

- Weigh the truth; take a reality check.

- Read sacred texts.

- Recite verbal affirmations, quotes, or slogans.

- Pray.

- Ask for what you need.

- Review self-knowledge tools, such as your temperament assessment and identity statement to renew your belief in your abilities and value.

- Recite your identity statement.

The Listen to Your Self Strategy

Like any relationship, the relationship you create with your Self requires conversation. Intuition is often thought to be the voice of Self. Imagine an enduring relationship without conversation. It would be ineffective. The quality of your relationship can be high and enriching, or not, depending on how well developed your awareness of internal conversation is, and how willing you are to give it attention.

Conversation happens internally, within your body, mind, spirit, and soul. The elements of soul and spirit are elusive, so for our purposes we will just say that both are fascinating conversationalists. While they are mysterious, they are actually quite intelligible. As we mentioned earlier, we have internal alarms that go off when we're operating at a loss of integrity, when all systems aren't operating as they should be—balanced, vital, and fully functioning. The alarms are symptoms of leaving congruency and entering disorder. Your Self will speak up in alarm.

How else does your Self speak to you? In the western world, the most accepted form of communication is physical. As you no doubt know, many fields of research connect physical conditions as cues, or messages, the body is giving to its owner. Your itchy,

burning eyes are your body saying, "Something in your environment is not good for you." Your tired, blistered feet are telling
you, "Take a rest," or, "Buy better fitting shoes." Listening for
and respecting these cues builds your relationship with your Self,
as it would if you were to listen to and respect the messages of
any friend. In many cultures throughout the world, respect for
the communication between one's mind, soul, and spirit is better
developed.

There may be a question as to the location of intuition, but
what is seldom disputed is its presence and its value. Even so,
many people shut off access to it. This would be like roping off
the services of a highly intelligent consultant from your life. We
encourage you to put your intuition to work for you, whether
you usually listen to your intuition or not.

If you doubt the validity of internal conversation, consider
this familiar scene. Harold is reading this book. He gets to the
part about the immature defense mechanism—denial. Within him
is a spark of recognition. It is his conscience saying, "You do this,
Harold. You're in denial over the way you exaggerate." His body
confirms the message by sending him a knot in his stomach. His
denial is activated and declares, "No way." In his mind, he hears
his mother, who handed down the pattern of denial to him and
whose voice is embedded in his original distorted belief, say,
"What's the problem with lying sometimes to save a little pain?"

Then it's Harold's turn to respond. If he pays attention to
the cues from his Self, identifies denial as an internal resistor no
longer out for his good, and gets rid of it, he will experience a
new peace and an improvement in his physical condition. The
knot in his stomach will go away, and he will face his problem
so that he can change it. If, on the other hand, he disregards the
cues from his Self, and instead lets denial continue, he will remain
in his distracted, partially honest life.

Your Self can be trusted; your thinking errors cannot be
trusted because they are lies. Picture them as blankets covering
your Self; as you remove them, your Self will be free to serve
you in a full, communicating relationship as your loving servant.
In the meantime, and even right now, invite your intuition to
guide you to truth. Notice the clues it gives you, speak back to
it by respecting it, loving it, and following its lead. You will become more whole as you merge your actions with your intuition.
Not doing this is turning your back on what many consider your
greatest resource.

The Counseling Strategy

Counseling can be an outstanding strategy for change. Getting a trained assistant to join you on your path to changing distorted beliefs can accelerate your effort and help you sort through your beliefs with added confidence. Here are things we want you to know when you seek counseling:

- You are in charge of your own developmental path.

- You have hired a counselor to serve you.

- If you're unhappy with the way the counselor is serving you, or feel uncomfortable for any reason, you may seek another. Counselors are just people. You will like some, and not others.

- If you find yourself in a pattern of dismissing counselors, you may be being driven by a thinking error or defense mechanism, particularly if the counselors are giving you similar information.

- Family and friends will have differing opinions about counselors, and even about the counselor you are seeing. Be open but not obligated to take their advice.

- Be specific with your counselor about what you are seeking.

- Do not feel that you will shock the counselor with the truth or that you will be perceived as crazy or a basketcase if you have problems. Because counselors are people, they can relate to having personal issues and behaviors that have caused difficulties.

When you call for an appointment with a counselor, be ready to describe your situation and your needs. Here are some phrases you may want to use. Feel free to tailor them to your needs.

- My family/friends/boss say I am in denial.

- I am being plagued by an overall sense of guilt and shame.

- I keep bumping up against the same mistakes and losses.

- I feel like the bottom of my life has fallen out.

- I want to identify why I have difficulty establishing long-term relationships.

- I want to understand why my opinion of myself and the opinions of others about me are so different.

- I want to take ownership of my life more seriously.

- I want to increase my sense of worth.

- I want to create a personal boundary system.

- I want to rid myself of thinking errors.

- I find myself wanting to hide, or feeling embarrassed.

The Journaling Strategy

Journaling takes many forms, and it is a tried-and-true tool for change. If you choose to use this strategy on your path to change, we urge you to think through possibilities that may sabotage your efforts. Do you enjoy writing out your thoughts and activities? Do you feel intimidated because you think you have to fill up the whole book? Do you feel guilty when you miss an entry? Do you worry that someone will read it? Once you determine what inhibits you from successful journaling, you can strategize ways to counter these fears. For example, if you feel guilty when you miss an entry, purchase a journal without dates so you don't feel distressed by an empty page. If you are intimidated by the idea of having to fill up a book, write your entries on individual sheets of paper and drop them in a journal box. If you worry that someone will read it, lock it in a special place and then when you're done with it, burn it. You can find a way. On at least some part of your treasuring path, journaling is worth using.

As we have said, there are many forms of journaling. We suggest you consider using David Burns' "Daily Mood Log," as it is a powerful way to recognize your misbeliefs, and clear them out. We highly recommend it as an important strategy that can eventually lead you to incorporating the process into your internal pattern of thinking, making it unnecessary to journal on paper if you prefer.

"The Daily Mood Log" works this way.

1. Log an upsetting event and the feelings or mood it produced.

2. Rate your feeling state on a scale of 1–10.

3. Identify what automatic thoughts came to you.

4. Use your knowledge of thinking errors and defenses and identify the error in your automatic thought.

5. Substitute the irrational, automatic thought with a rational, intentional one.

Here is an example:

The upsetting event: I was afraid to speak to a woman at a club.

Emotion: Anxious

Rate of feeling state: 8 on a scale of 1–10

Automatic thought: I'm not attractive enough.

Distortion: Fortune-telling, mind reading, all-or-nothing thinking

Substituted rational thoughts: I may not be unusually attractive, but I look okay and there might be a certain chemistry between us.

If you did not have an understanding of thinking errors and defenses, you would be in the dark about confidently identifying them. This is an excellent example of the value of knowledge. Now that you do understand them, you can readily recognize them in yourself. The knowledge you have gained in this book and through other sources will be valuable in making your mood journal a belief-altering activity.

The Pros and Cons Strategy

Perhaps the most common and popular strategy to make decisions is the simple chart listing the "pros and cons" of a choice or situation. It's logical and usually points to a clear choice. We believe it's also a helpful strategy for identifying and changing your beliefs. It requires that you are open to the truth when you see it clearly written down. You may want to use a change helper in this activity if you find it difficult to see the "cons."

The example on the following page illustrates the usefulness of this strategy:

The Belief I Wish to Change:

I believe I am bound to mess up, no matter what I try.

Pros (Why I hang on to these faulty beliefs)	**Cons** (Why I should go against these faulty beliefs)
I don't have to try.	Discounts my true capabilities and reduces my importance.
People won't expect things from me if I don't try.	It isn't true; I have succeeded at plenty of things.
I won't be as disappointed when I fail.	I feel good when I demonstrate competence.
People will take care of me.	I am energized by contributing to the good of others and myself.
I don't have to be responsible.	I'm sick and tired of feeling like a screwup, and others are tired of me behaving like one.

After filling out this pros and cons chart, you might conclude, "Being a screwup keeps me a spectator rather than an active participant in life. I've been a spectator long enough." (Other possible conclusions: "Believing I am a screwup is a symptom of me sabotaging myself and shortchanging my opportunities"; "Believing I am a screwup is standing between me and my dreams.")

The Acquiring a Change Helper Strategy

When some people think of acquiring a change helper, they look to the people closest to them. This may or may not be a good idea for a number of reasons, one being that those closest to you may be "helping" you stay right where you are in your distorted self-view and boundaries. Also, they may be afraid to help you grow out of fear that you may change, or out of their desire to protect you from what they see as discomfort. Another reason you may want to avoid using a change helper that is close to you is that they may have labeled you as "the one who's always available,"or "the one who's fragile," and may be unable to release you from that script. So, we suggest you follow these guidelines in selecting your change helper(s). They must be able to

- Honor you by keeping a confidence.

- Speak the truth with respect.

- Practice the qualities you seek.

- Support you without controlling you.

- Remain a "consultant" rather than a "manager."

- Accept your leadership in your own change process.

- Respect your rights to your own opinions, values, and choices.

- Listen well.

The Visualization Strategy

Visualization is a powerful tool for change. It's a service of your imagination, one of those built-in friends waiting to help you. It works in cooperation with the rest of you, ready to assist you in changing your false beliefs and defeating behaviors. If you are unfamiliar with the practice of visualization, you may want to seek reputable resources to determine how it can best help you. One book we have enjoyed is *In The Mind's Eye* by Arnold Lazarus. It's full of examples of actual methods and case studies where visualization successfully helps people overcome damaging fears, beliefs, and behaviors. The book is written to be used with or without a counselor. In it, Lazarus writes, "Some people seem to have much greater will power than others. They can refuse tempting foods, quit smoking, and generally avoid indulging in various excesses and bad habits. I believe that these so-called strong-willed people are able to break bad habits, not because of some inner 'strength' per se, but because they have a well-defined image of the negative consequences." He believes people who have difficulty ending defeating behaviors are not weak, but simply visualize the pleasures, rather than the negative consequences, of their choices.

Here are three visualizations related to changing your beliefs about your treasuredness:

- Visualize a line drawn between you and a particular thinking error. Let it represent your unwillingness to let the thinking error influence you.

- Visualize yourself as the ruby slippers, protected from harm by a display case you have constructed. You hold the keys to the case and can open and close it depending on who and what is near.

- Visualize your Self separate and free from your misbeliefs, thinking errors, and defenses. Maybe your Self is on one side of a gate, and your misbeliefs are on the other side in the form of garbage. Picture yourself setting them out to be picked up on garbage day.

Visualization can just as easily occur on a busy street corner as it can while you are quietly sitting in a comfortable chair with soft music playing. Rather than a mysterious and monklike activity, it's a powerful tool for people on the go and at rest. In fact, it's particularly helpful in "carrying you away" in the heat of life's battles to center yourself and stay on your chosen path as your own best friend. As Arnold Lazarus says, "If you practice something in imagination, it is bound to have an effect on the real situation."

The Countering Strategy

Countering is another one of those logical solutions that people often do naturally. It is simply countering, or substituting, a negative thought, belief, or behavior with one that is good for you. Countering techniques for changing your beliefs could include:

When your internal resistor tells you:	You might counter it by:
You can't walk your two miles today because it's raining.	Laughing at your insinuation that you aren't waterproof, then put on your rain gear and go.
Your family probably thinks your a lousy cook because you forgot to buy rolls for the birthday dinner last night.	Saying, "Forgetting to buy rolls has nothing to do with being a good or lousy cook." Concentrate on what went well, then buy a supply of rolls and keep them in the freezer so it doesn't happen again.
You are doomed to staying in your job forever because you didn't get the promotion.	Reminding yourself that staying in your job forever will be your choice, not someone else's. Determine why you didn't get the promotion. If it's something you can correct or learn, do it. If not, continue developing as an excellent, noticeable employee—there or elsewhere.

We recommend you prepare yourself for successful countering by arranging some countering tools.

- Put your shoes in a closet by the door so you can slip into them for a spontaneous walk to shift your thoughts and attention.

- Place books you especially love, particularly those with positive quotes or poetry, in a spot you can access quickly to replace negative thoughts.

- Place a stack of notecards with stamped envelopes and your address book in a ready location to write encouragements to people. Keep adding to your list of people you will write to when you are tempted to believe your life is useless or uninspiring.

- Call people to say hello or thanks. This is where voice mail is effective. You can say what you want to say, add "No need to call me back," and hang up!

- Keep your bike or skates ready for a quick spin to counter beliefs that you are boring or lazy.

- Record your own set of countering music from CDs and tapes. Let the music emotionally charge you to counter negative beliefs. Do the same with videos.

- Memorize an inspiring poem or adopt a personal set of memorized quotes or sacred text to repeat to yourself.

Earlier in the book we referred to a situation where a woman refused a dance with an unpleasant person when before she would have agreed to it. She came to the decision by countering—substituting one belief for another—which led her to new behavior. The thought process might have gone like this:

She was asked to dance by a man she found to be unpleasant. Her initial thought was, "Oh no, I'm going to feel uncomfortable through the whole dance!" She then countered this thought by creating a boundary that was an act of treasuring herself. Her next thought was, "I don't have to do something that will make me feel uncomfortable. I'll politely but firmly say 'no'."

But then beliefs and influencers started entering her mind. Her mom always said, "Be nice. Don't hurt the poor man's feelings." Her sister said, "Good grief, it's only one dance, not a lifetime. Give the guy a thrill." A distorted core belief said, "I am unkind if I refuse to dance with someone who asks, so I should dance with this man even though I prefer not to."

Like a best friend, however, her new core belief stepped up and countered with truth, "I can be selective about who I dance with." She listened to this truth, set the other beliefs aside, and concluded that this man "is not someone I want to be close to, even for five minutes."

This conscious countering will become familiar to you as you adopt new beliefs about yourself and your personal value. Old false beliefs will step up and try to influence you to return to familiar patterns and weak boundaries, but as you replace the false beliefs with new ones, your ability to make choices based on truth will become what's most familiar and natural.

Now you have a dozen new strategies to integrate into your overall plan of changing your beliefs and treasuring yourself. Which ones will you integrate into your program of change? Who will your change helper be? When will you begin? It's up to you.

By the way, how would a best friend behave in the throes of the kinds of change you're seeking? Patient, enthused, encouraging, understanding, truth-speaking, and proud. We encourage you to adopt this attitude toward yourself regardless of what anyone else in your life is saying and doing to you.

Reminding Yourself

- You will naturally formulate your own program of change.

- Adjusting the way you think is your stepping stone to improved living.

- The four ingredients to growth and transformation are: knowledge that changing is a process, structuring your environment for change, using interventions and theories, and preventing relapse or loss of insight.

- Progressing from change to change puts you on an upward spiral.

- If you want to get good at being your own best friend, you must become good at the process of change.

- As you make changes, be gentle and friendly toward yourself.

- Intervention strategies will help you when your boundaries are challenged.

10

Getting to Know and Like Yourself

A lifestyle of friendship with yourself contains many vital elements. This chapter begins with forgiving yourself, because trying to build a relationship with someone you haven't yet forgiven destines the friendship to trouble.

Imagine yourself confident and secure with clearly set boundaries, and there you are, standing with your suit jacket over your shoulder talking to an associate. You say, "I am my own best friend, that's why." You're answering the question, "What enables you to set such effective boundaries?" You're someone who has made friends with yourself and the friendship has become a lifestyle.

Forgiving Yourself

Getting beyond regretting your mistakes is essential to personal freedom. It's also crucial to becoming your own best friend. What does it matter if others forgive you if you don't forgive you? Everyone else aside, you are alone with yourself and your unforgiveness. This can be a sad existence for you distracted by fear, regret, sabotage, lost joy, and captivity.

Many people find it difficult to forgive themselves for mistakes they have made, losses they have incurred, and opportunities they have missed. This is particularly true when misbeliefs, thinking errors, and defense mechanisms are operating unrestrained. After all, these are internal resistors to truth, they are lies that produce distorted conclusions and behaviors, including the inability to forgive.

At the root of many people's difficulty in forgiving themselves is an unwillingness to accept their humanity, to accept the fact that they are imperfect. It would be like a cat unable to forgive itself for eating the family hamster. Cats eat rodents, sometimes they mistakenly eat one that is off-limits. As upsetting as it is, that's what cats do. And as upsetting as it is, you are bound to make mistakes and must forgive yourself if you're to thrive.

Not forgiving yourself is like falling into the mud and conducting life from there instead of stepping out onto clean, dry land. It doesn't work, and it makes everything messy. What are some things people have trouble forgiving themselves for?

- Not knowing

- Knowing and not doing, or doing it anyway

- Not resisting enough

- Not doing enough

- Not seeing

- Not understanding

- Being selfish

- Using people

- Letting themselves be used

- Manipulating people and situations

- Letting themselves be manipulated

- Having to always be right

- Advancing themselves at the expense of others

- Not trusting their instincts

- Not being true to themselves

- Being influenced by someone else's identity instead of living out their own

- Trusting untrustworthy authorities

- Coercing others to follow

- Not being an advocate for someone who needed them

- Not getting out of an abusive relationship or job sooner

- Not seizing opportunities

- Believing lies

- Letting someone else's preferences dominate their own

- Not being a better child, parent, spouse, friend, sister, brother, employee, student

And the list goes on.

Everyone shares a universal need for self-forgiveness. Your ability to forgive yourself will depend on who you are. Your temperament, upbringing, spiritual beliefs, emotional and mental development, self-view, and understanding of perfection versus excellence will all determine your ability to forgive yourself. A brief look at each of these contributing factors may help you understand your personal challenges, or lack of them, in forgiving yourself.

Self-Forgiveness and Your Temperament

You will recall that your temperament reveals itself in your set of preferences when dealing with people and situations. It is your built-in response system. Therefore, your temperament will have a preferred response to handling mistakes and forgiveness. Generally, here's how your various preferences might respond to the decision to forgive yourself:

Introvert: "I'd prefer to have some time to think about my past and my self-forgiveness option. I may or may not talk to anyone else about this private matter."

Extrovert: "I'd prefer to talk through all this forgiveness stuff with some others."

Sensor: "When I am convinced that forgiving myself is a practical response to my past mistakes, I'll do it."

Intuitive: "I've grappled with my past mistakes and in my gut I've come to know that I should forgive myself."

Thinker: "To forgive myself makes sense. For me to be more focused and productive I will forgive myself."

Feeler: "I hate feeling the guilt and shame associated with this unfinished business—self-forgiveness is my path to peace."

Perceiver: "I'm not sure if forgiving myself is the best way to deal with my past mistakes. I'll keep my options open for now."

Judger: "I really want to get some closure on the past. I'm ready *now* to forgive myself."

Self-Forgiveness and Your Upbringing

You first learned to deal with mistakes, bad choices, and forgiveness at home with your primary caregivers. If apologies and forgiveness were a way of life, you may be able to forgive yourself quite easily. If not, and you haven't acquired the skill through intentional effort or through the modeling in a new relationship, you may lack experience in this vital self-nurturing behavior. In a nutshell, here are the basic parenting styles and their typical approach to mistakes and forgiveness:

Authoritarian: "If you would have done what I said in the first place you wouldn't be in this mess."

Permissive: "Do whatever seems right for you to be okay."

Ambivalent: "I suppose you could forgive yourself but that doesn't mean it all goes away."

Democratic: "We all make mistakes, and we all have the option to forgive ourselves. This choice is yours."

Self-Forgiveness and Your Spiritual Beliefs

Your faith can be very influential in your attitude toward forgiving yourself. You may either feel that God is forgiving or else unforgiving, and that may influence your attitude toward self-forgiveness.

Self-Forgiveness and Your
Emotional and Mental Development

Emotional maturity helps you put your mistakes and bad choices in perspective, deal with them, and move on. It also enables you to take responsibility for yourself and your actions, and reject false guilt. Emotional immaturity impedes progress, it causes you to avoid taking responsibility for your mistakes, and, if guilt for a mistake is accepted, emotional immaturity can cause you to hold on to it too long. Your ability to engage in self-talk based on truth is a sign of mature mental development and will enable you to forgive yourself using strategies such as countering. Countering involves arguing or disputing your irrational thoughts with the truth. The false beliefs, such as, "I'm unforgivable," become weaker as they are argued against.

Self-Forgiveness and Your Self-View

A truth-based self-view will enable you to see yourself as flawed yet competent. It will let you be human and protect you from believing you are mistake-proof. If this is your self-view, your inner belief, you will give yourself freedom to choose incorrectly, and forgive yourself for it. If this is not your self-view, you will have difficulty forgiving yourself and will experience the loss that goes with it.

Self-Forgiveness and Your Understanding
of Perfectionism Versus Excellence

What do you believe about the difference between perfectionism and excellence? Your answer reveals your inner belief about your standards for yourself. If your standards are unrealistic, your failure will be hard to swallow—and forgive. A perfectionist is different than someone who strives for and produces excellence. A perfectionist is usually driven by a *need* to be perfect and produce perfectly. A person who strives for excellence does so for the personal or professional pride in it, and for the experience of knowing the best possible job has been done with the time, tools, or budget available. Many people who do excellent work struggle with being a perfectionist. You can tell which you are by how you feel when you miss the mark of perfection. Do you incriminate yourself? Replay the imperfection? Become blocked by it? Judge yourself unfairly? An ability to let go of your perfectionism will help you forgive yourself for your inevitable mistakes.

Using Your Concluding Lens As a Self-Forgiveness Tool

It can also be helpful to run the idea of forgiving yourself through the concluding lenses we discussed in chapter 6, especially your preferred lens. You might be concluding things about yourself in different ways—perhaps some of these lenses will ring true for you. Here are various possible concluding lenses:

Forgiveness through the Authority Lens

I can forgive myself because

- The church says that I should (religious authority).

- The Bible says that I should (religious authority).

- My sacred writing or spiritual leaders say that I should (spiritual authority).

- My psychiatrist/physician says that it's in my best interest (medical authority).

- My counselor/therapist says that it's in my best interest (psychological authority).

- My teacher/professor/mentor told me it was best (educational authority).

Forgiveness through the Emotional Lens

I can forgive myself because

- I feel freed up and better when I forgive other people, and I will no doubt feel better when I forgive myself.

- I am tired of feeling guilty and I am ready to be free of it.

- I will feel so good when this guilt is off my back.

Forgiveness through the Sense/Experience Lens

I can forgive myself because

- I have experienced forgiving myself.

- I have felt what it is like to be forgiven.

- I have heard the words of forgiveness spoken.

- I have felt the hug of forgiveness and I know forgiving myself is in my best interest.

Forgiveness through the Intuition Lens

I can forgive myself because

- I have grappled with this matter and I have come to know in the depth of my being that I will never be able to move on until I forgive myself.

- I just know it's wise to forgive myself.

Forgiveness through the Scientific Lens

I can forgive myself because

- I gathered all the facts, sorted and studied them, and I came to see the merit of self-forgiveness.

- I thought through the logical implications of forgiving myself, and finally, I experimented by forgiving myself and evaluating the outcome.

- Evidence of the outcome of forgiving myself for past mistakes clearly shows that it is in my best interest.

Forgiveness through the Logic Lens

I can forgive myself because

- Not forgiving imperfect people for their imperfections doesn't make sense.

- Since I am an imperfect person who has made mistakes, forgiving myself makes sense, too.

Understanding the Benefits of Forgiving Yourself

If you're still unconvinced about the importance of forgiving yourself, read the following benefits.

- An intimate, appreciative relationship with yourself will be restored.

- The energy expended on self-incrimination can be redirected to life-enriching activities.

- You will be fully present to enjoy significant, authentic interactions with people in genuine community, rather than living in partial presence, distracted by your guilt and fear.

- You will be known for who you really are, enjoying an enhanced integrity that embraces your whole self.

- You will come to terms with the past and let it be the past.

- You will become less critical of yourself and others as you recognize, and forgive, the universality of human imperfection.

- You will reduce the stress and secondary stress-related symptoms associated with self-blame or self-contempt.

- You will promote harmony within yourself.

- You will model for others, especially children, that you can fail and not be a failure.

- You will be demonstrating maturity when you take responsibility for your behavior, forgive yourself, and let go of self-blame.

- If you're a person whose faith encourages you to forgive yourself, you will be employing a practice consistent with your religious teachings and beliefs.

Not Forgiving Yourself

Here is what you can expect if you do not forgive yourself:

- You will prevent yourself from operating from a place of personal confidence, peace, and self-respect.

- You will promote shame and self-contempt within your Self.

- You will limit your honest, intimate presence with others.

- You will limit, or put a lid on, your joy.

- You will be sapped of motivation and drive.

- You may experience unnecessary stress-related illnesses.

- You will be normalizing self-blame as an accepted attitude for your children or others in your life.

- You will remain stuck—and tired.

Ceremoniously Forgiving Yourself

If you wish, and when you're ready, lead yourself in a ceremony of forgiveness alone or with a trusted friend. It can be anything you want it to be. Include these essentials:

- A time for you to state what remains unforgiven within you

- A confirmation statement of your forgiveness

- A symbol of your self-forgiveness

Forgiveness is an ongoing gift that will allow you to keep self-blame and contempt out of your life.

Renewing a Relationship with Yourself

What you will be doing as you continue the process of setting boundaries by treasuring yourself is establishing a new relationship with yourself. It will be a wonderful time of ongoing discovery. You will find positive things about yourself that you had overlooked. You will be open to receiving love and praise from others and you will be ready to pursue relationships and opportunities that help you fulfill your dreams and purpose. You will step onto a learning track that keeps you growing, improving, and developing your talents, increasing the tools you have to use in living out your authentic self. Plus, you will learn to be easier on yourself, as you would be to someone you adore. Yet your gentleness toward yourself will not be an excuse for laziness or a lack of excellence. Because the love and trust for yourself will be growing, you will be able to more accurately evaluate what's going on in your life. You will become your own invaluable truth-teller. In a real sense, you will follow the steps to any healthy and intimate relationship.

When you enter into a relationship with someone, you usually follow a predictable pattern.

- You chat.

- You share facts.

- You voice opinions.

- You reveal beliefs.

- You declare core passions.

In the same way, as you renew your relationship with yourself, you will move through similar stages of discovery—but it will be about you. You will listen to yourself talk and decide what you think of the way you verbally express yourself. You will learn to talk less or more, or more interestingly. You will learn more facts about yourself, your preferences, your talents, your goals, dreams, and purpose. You will adopt opinions about new things and voice them more confidently when the time seems right. You will declare your passion to yourself first, and then to the world—again, when the time is right. This is what it means to be your own best friend.

A healthy, intimate relationship involves two people who value one another, tell the truth, assume the best, want the best, stimulate, inspire, and believe. This is the relationship you will have between you and yourself as you choose to treasure yourself. From this place of treasuredness you can confidently enter situations in life that require effective boundaries.

What stage of relationship would you say you are in with your Self? Look at this list and think about it:

- **Level One:** Chatting, light conversation. *You are just getting to know yourself.*

- **Level Two:** Sharing facts. *You know basic facts about yourself.*

- **Level Three:** Voicing opinions. *You have strong opinions.*

- **Level Four:** Revealing beliefs. *You know your beliefs.*

- **Level Five:** Declaring core passions. *You know your core passions.*

Knowing Yourself

What is there to know about yourself? Obviously there is more than we can list here, but this is a start. These are examples of ways that you know yourself.

Ethnic origins

Temperament

Learning style

Allergies

Physical capacities

Creative strengths

Self-nurturing capabilities

Energizers

Network of advocates and mentors

What you need to feel comfortable in social situations

What you need to feel confident at work

What you need to motivate you to persevere

Your intrinsic motivators

Your emotional range

Your medical history

Your biorhythms

What lighting you prefer

What décor pleases you

Your favorite books

Your favorite movies

Your favorite tools

Your favorite people

Your favorite songs and artists

What you need to feel honored and celebrated sexually

What kind of friend you want to be

Your purpose

What kind of doctors you prefer

Your issues

What kind of difference you want to make

Where you're strong

Where you need to grow

Your integrity

Your favorite places

What makes you laugh

What inspires you to do your best

What hinders you from doing your best

What your love language is

What feeds your emotions

How you cope with loss

Your guiding values

What feeds your soul

What immobilizes you

Your sense of humor

What scares you or causes you dread	What you need in a caring relationship	Gift-giving style
What stimulates your mind	How you confront	Wardrobe preferences
How your intuition works	How you like to be confronted	Spiritual orientation
	What you need to be successful at work	Your communication style
		Your sensuality

There. That should get you started. Richard Brodie, in his book *Getting Past OK*, says it well.

> Before I made the decision to trust my own judgment about how to live my life, I searched long and hard for an answer, for someone else to tell me how I *should* live it. I was hungry for advice, and the more I got, the more confused I became. I tried to be like my role models, to copy the way they acted and talked because it was clear to me they were powerful, fulfilled people. I copied their actions, but the real secret of their success never occurred to me: in those qualities that I admired and in those areas where they succeeded, *they trusted their own judgment.* I saw they were confident, so I acted confident—but that didn't get me the fulfillment I saw in them. They really *were* confident, because they trusted themselves. I saw they were sure of what they wanted, so I set my sights on the same kinds of things they wanted—but that didn't get me fulfillment. They really *wanted* those things and they knew they wanted them, because they trusted themselves.

Trusting the Treasured Self

Sometimes it's easier to trust yourself *before* you face who you are and how you think rather than *after*. It can feel like finding out a friend has led a secret life. Before knowing your misbeliefs, you could trust yourself without thinking about it. Now, you know the truth and the truth is you have made choices that haven't always been in your best interest. The reasons for those choices have been due to faulty or outdated ways of thinking and concluding. How do you now learn to trust your treasured self like you would trust a proven best friend? You do what you do with a new friend, you gradually learn to love and trust one another as your relationship develops.

It can be a jolting experience to realize you have not always made choices to be your own best friend, that what you believed to be the truth, was actually distorted, that you manipulated your destiny, and/or lived behind a false self. Most people ask, "How could I have done this to myself?" It's common to question yourself for a while, once you realize how easy it is to let your guard down and allow self-defeating choices in. As you become more aware of your old thinking patterns and move into authentic living, however, you will grow in trust and confidence.

Stacey, for example, used to use her credit card "without thinking" to purchase merchandise on home shopping networks and infomercials. She believed she was making good choices. As she got to know herself, however, she realized that she bought more things when she was feeling overwhelmed by too many responsibilities. It wasn't really merchandise she was buying, it was emotional relief. She wasn't enjoying her life, so she found pleasure in the deliveries.

When Stacey looked at why her life was overwhelming, she discovered she was agreeing to things she couldn't comfortably fit into her schedule in order to uphold her image as "the woman who can do it all." She had embedded this image into her identity and was now trapped in it. To say, "Sorry, I can't," would mean she wasn't the woman who can do it all. What would her image be then?

As Stacey discovered her misbelief, she went through a period of not trusting her choices. This is very normal, and, in fact, is healthy. It causes us to look closely at why we do what we do and seek help when we need it. Stacey learned to recognize her need to shop as a sign that something was wrong. Before she picked up the phone to the shopping networks, if she thought she might be in denial, she would call a friend who would help her sort things out. She became adept at using her stand-in symbol (her childhood friend, Missy) and often asked herself, "Would I advise Missy to order this now?" This equipped Stacey to learn to treat herself as she would want Missy to be treated. In this way Stacey was able to learn treasuring self-behaviors that eventually led to an ability to reduce her need to take on extra responsibilities. She could then work at a controllable and satisfying level.

The Steps toward Trust

If you have an effective boundary system in place, you will not quickly trust people with priceless things like your body, soul, and mind. You will test people's trustworthiness over time to see if you are willing to share your treasured self in a relationship with them. After all, you don't leave your car unlocked in a big city with the keys in it, you don't leave your front door ajar, and you don't leave your purse or wallet on a park bench while you take a walk. Why, then, would you carelessly leave yourself open to untrustworthy people? You wouldn't. Not if you treasured your self like you do your car, house, or money.

How do you rebuild trust in yourself when you realize you've hurt yourself in the past? You do it step by step and you do it gently, without ridicule. Here's how Celia regained trust in herself after realizing she had spent a lifetime sabotaging her own success.

Pattern of self-sabotage

Celia's steps to regaining trust:

1. Acknowledged past sabotages as history rather than incrimination

2. Declared a belief in her ability to care for herself

3. Added a "pause" step into her process of making choices

4. Asked herself regularly, "Is this in my best interest?"

5. Evaluated each small step of a situation, project, or relationship to determine whether to continue or end it

These steps to rebuilding trust with yourself are similar to the development of any relationship that leads to intimacy. You will trust yourself in small things and gradually believe in yourself enough to confidently trust your choices. Not only that, but you will also have created a support system around you with at least one other person who can help when needed. In reality, you have never been in a better position to trust yourself because you are facing truth about yourself, you're making adjustments, and seeking help in your journey to owning and treasuring your life.

Making Friends with Your Whole Self

Just as people tend to associate with a certain group of people and not others, they can become good friends with certain parts of themselves and ignore others. This inner clique, so to speak, can put a lid on a person's development as a whole person. You own all of your parts, and they need your attention and love. Debrena Jackson Gandy, in her book *Sacred Pampering Principles*, explains,

> Once when I was leading a love-relationships workshop, I stopped to ask the group of women, "What kind of things would you do if you were in love with the most wonderful person in the world?" After a few second of silence while they contemplated the question, women started to raise their hands to respond. As I went around the room calling on women, they shouted out all kinds of delicious and exciting possibilities including candlelight dinners, reading poetry, massages, long Sunday-afternoon drives, walks on the beach, and love letters. At the end of this outpouring of responses I told them that the most wonderful person in the world was sitting in their own seats. I told them that they would be looking her in the face if they were to look in the mirror. They were speechless.

Making Friends with Your Body

How friendly do you feel toward your body? How good a friend have you been to it? Do you like it? Do you appreciate what it does for you? Do you present it in ways that show you care about it? Do you pay attention to its needs? Do you do your best to prevent it from disease, tiredness, distress?

Creating a positive, friendly relationship with your body is an act of friendship toward yourself. Some people do it easily, others don't. Most people land somewhere in between. Assess your level of body friendliness and take steps to become your body's best friend. There are many wonderful books, videos, and programs today that can give you direction in caring for your body. When put in a context of being your body's best friend, common health and fitness strategies take on a new meaning. Here are some tips to remind you how to be your body's friend:

- **Feed your body things that are good for it.** Why would you intentionally make a friend sick?

- **Take your body to the doctor and dentist for checkups.** What kind of friend would ignore basic care?

- **Keep your body flexible and strong.** What kind of friend would want you rigid and weak?

- **Appreciate your body's contribution to your life.** What kind of friend would never say "thanks"?

- **Respond to your body when it is sick or stressed.** What kind of friend would ignore a call for help?

- **Present your body to its best advantage.** What kind of friend would make you look bad?

- **Respect your body's design and rhythm.** What kind of friend would disrespect your individual qualities?

- **Give your body a break.** What kind of friend doesn't let you rest?

- **Challenge your body to accomplish new things.** What kind of friend doesn't want you to grow and develop?

- **Give your body pleasure.** What kind of friend withholds what pleases you?

Making Friends with Your Mind

How friendly do you feel toward your mind? How good a friend have you been to your intellect? Do you like how it works for you? Do you enjoy the way it furnishes you with the ideas you need? Do you know and appreciate its style of learning new things?

Creating a positive, friendly relationship with your mind is also an act of treasuring yourself. As Howard Clinebell writes in *Wellbeing*, "The dual keys to maximizing love-centered well-being in your whole life are the health and aliveness of your mind and the health and aliveness of your spirit." You may want to spend some time evaluating your relationship with your mind and make appropriate adjustments or advancements in your care and appreciation of it.

The following suggestions can help you become your mind's best friend:

- **Fill your mind with good information.** What kind of friend treats you badly then expects you to treat them well?

- **Get to know how your own mind works.** What kind of friend doesn't want to know what makes you tick?

- **Challenge your mind to realistic new accomplishments.** What kind of friend doesn't push you to realize a new perspective?

- **Stimulate your mind with new information.** What kind of friend bores you with the same old stuff?

- **Trust that your mind is capable of figuring out what you need.** What kind of friend doesn't do what they can to help?

- **Exercise your mind to keep it in shape.** What kind of friend doesn't want you fit?

- **Supply your mind with necessary nourishments.** What kind of friend withholds healthy input?

- **Play with your mind.** What kind of friend doesn't have fun with you?

Making Friends with Your Spirit

How friendly do you feel toward your spirit? Some people believe that your spirit is your deepest self, the most inner part of you. Muriel and John James, in their book, *Passion for Life: Psychology and the Human Spirit*, describe "spirit" in this way, "The human spirit is the vital animating force in a person that can move a person beyond the normal confines of life to a sense of wholeness and holiness. As a vital force, it is alive within each of us; as an animating force, it moves us to action ... This spiritual self is universal because it is common to all. Yet, it is also personal as each of us expresses it in our unique way."

Letting your spirit express itself in your life is an act of profound friendliness to yourself. You can't touch your spirit like you can touch your leg, but spirit can be felt and known. It's about the essentials of life rather than the superficials, and when you feel empty or ask "Is this all there is?" it is your spirit you are feeling and hearing. Many people equate spirit with religious beliefs, and certainly your faith is centered in your spirit. Yet spirit, in the context of this discussion, is the *core essential* of what has meaning to you. When your life lacks meaning, your spirit becomes malnourished and hungry. You can feel the hunger in your spirit in much the same way you feel hunger in your stomach, and you can feed your spirit in real ways to satisfy that hunger—or not, depending on how good a friend you choose to be to yourself.

Here are some ways to become your own spirit's best friend:

- **Decide what is most important to you in life and satisfy your appetite for it.** What kind of friend would withhold what you most want?

- **Develop a way of seeing life that keeps you appreciative.** What kind of friend wouldn't point out the beauty or truth of a situation?

- **Seek expression of your faith in ways that bring you joy and nurture.** What kind of friend would want you to hold in your deep beliefs?

- **Surround yourself with symbols of what your spirit loves.** What kind of friend wouldn't help you remember what you love?

Making Friends with Your Self-Expressions

How friendly do you feel toward the way you express yourself? Self-expression includes things like your talents, goals, contributions, creativity, and style. Becoming your own best friend includes embracing the outward expressions of your inward identity. Self-expression is where the fun is; where your good ideas get to play, where your feelings speak, where your talents are displayed and developed, and where you offer yourself to the common good. It's a great place for a true friendship with yourself to thrive.

As you develop your self-expression, you will want to take full advantage of people, products, books, and tapes that can lead you in detail to a successful expression of your identity in all parts of your life. In the meantime, here are some ideas to get you started:

- **Dust off and develop talents you've ignored.** What kind of friend would keep gifts on the back shelf?

- **Align your goals with what means the most to you.** What kind of friend would let you set goals that aren't in tune with what you really want?

- **Ask yourself what you'd most like to do to help the world and then start doing it.** What kind of friend would ask you to contribute to the common good in ways you can't get fired up about?

- **Adjust your wardrobe, your home, your office, your bookshelf, your vacations, your car, your hobbies, your yard, your gift-giving, your stationery, and your traditions to your personal style.** What kind of friend would want to rob you of joy in the dailiness of life?

Making Friends with Your Emotions

You came into this world with a broader range of emotions than most people can imagine. According to Aphrodite Matsakis in *I Can't Get Over It, A Handbook for Trauma Survivors,* these are really just shades of four basic emotions: sadness, anger, joy, and fear. Emotions are your feelings. They are linked to beliefs and events. When a belief you hold encounters a situation or event, feelings are produced. For example, if you believe your sister is the favored one in the family and you discover your parents are visiting her, you may experience feelings of jealousy and resentment. Similarly, if you believe you're a good manager and you receive praise from your supervisor at a staff meeting, you may experience feelings of joy. Emotions, then, tell you that you have believed certain things and you have interpreted events in certain ways.

Emotions are a gift, and Leslie Cameron-Bandler and Michael Lebeau, authors of *The Emotional Hostage,* praise emotions as a source of "change, innovation, and fulfillment." You have emotional choice and, according to Cameron-Bandler and Lebeau, you can learn what each emotion is communicating to you.

Some people's range of emotion is narrow, limited to "fine," "okay," and "could be better." Other people are very expressive of the way they are feeling. Emotions are a gift. The question is, have you become friends with them? Here are some ways to become your emotions' best friend:

- **Let yourself feel your feelings fully without labeling them "right" or "wrong."** What kind of friend would short-change your emotions?

- **Once felt, let your feelings lead you back to their source (or, the underlying reason that you really feel the particular emotion) so you can learn more about yourself.** What kind of friend would say "no" to valuable information?

- **Learn to describe what you are feeling.** What kind of friend wouldn't help you understand what it is you're feeling?

- **Learn to ask for what you need to feel a certain way.** What kind of friend would ignore asking for something you need?

- **Learn what your emotions are trying to tell you.** What kind of friend wouldn't try to find out what you really mean?

These are the basics of being your own best friend. Now let's look at ways to reinforce your desire to treasure yourself through symbols.

Symbolizing the Treasured Self

There is power in symbolizing your internal decision to treasure yourself with external objects. Symbols are commonly used to remind us of people we love, beliefs we hold, and dreams we hope come true. A photograph is a symbol of people you love, a shell from a beach trip is a symbol of an especially good time with friends, and a collection of angels is a symbol of one's belief in divine care. There are many important points of life that can be strengthened with symbols, including your sense of treasuredness.

Selecting a symbol to represent being your own best friend will add one more layer to your resolve to own your life and set effective boundaries. It is a physical presence that calls you to stand firm in your choices. We have found it very helpful in our own lives and in the lives of our clients.

Reminder Symbols

A reminder symbol is any item that takes you back to a key experience or time when you chose to commit yourself to being your own best friend, owning your life, and/or setting better boundaries. It can be a silent, or not so silent, voice reminding you of something vital you have chosen to do or believe or become.

Melanie, a woman who at one time in her life felt trapped in an unhappy relationship, sent us a snapshot of a birdcage with an open door. Perched on top of the cage was a lovely imitation songbird. When Melanie found the cage, it was rusted and dirty, but she was moved by it in spite of its decaying appearance. It reminded her of the "caged" life she had led and she quickly adopted it as a symbol. She restored the cage and painted it, then left the cage door open to remind her that she is now flying free. It has become an important symbol and point of encouragement in her continued growth.

Melanie's birdcage reminds her of her freedom as owner of her life. It could be called a "reminder symbol." It can be a helpful tool.

The criteria for selecting your reminder symbol is simple. Choose an object that (1) pleases you, (2) makes sense to you even if it makes no sense to anyone else, and (3) works. You may even want several reminder symbols. The choice is yours, because just as you are in charge of your life, you are in charge of the type and number of reminders you have in your environment.

Examples of Reminder Symbols

Like stand-in symbols, reminder symbols are a personal, outward expression of something that has inner importance. As you collect reminders of your treasuredness, you will be visually surrounded by proof of your decision to own your life and set effective boundaries. The following are examples of reminder symbols others have used. Use the blanks provided to fill in some symbols of your own.

Reminder Symbols

Item	What It Symbolizes
Carousel horse	Permission to be childlike
Black-and-white framed photo of a fence	Importance of boundaries
Displayed collection of locks and keys	Ownership and boundaries
Picture of parent embracing a child	Treasuredness
Growing pile of small stones in decorative jar	Each stone is a symbol of a boundary set and kept
Silver locket with picture of self as a child	Treasuring yourself

Stand-In Symbols

In chapter 9, we discussed a stand-in strategy for making good choices as a responsible owner and boundary-setter for your life. The strategy simply means that when you have difficulty making a good choice for yourself, you insert another person, pet, or treasured object in your place, ask yourself, "What choice would I want them to make?" and then make that choice for yourself. Your stand-in symbol, then, would be a physical representation of that person, pet, or object. Ginger often used her daughter Kim as a stand-in treasure. A picture of Kim is her symbol. She wants Kim to make healthy, treasuring choices, so when Ginger is tempted to make an unhealthy choice, she looks at Kim's picture in her wallet and makes the choice that she knows would benefit Kim.

The criteria for selecting your stand-in symbol is that it must (1) be a person, pet, or object you value unconditionally, (2) evoke a protective, passionate emotion within you, and (3) awaken in you a deep longing for its/their very best interest.

Examples of Stand-In Symbols

Symbols are a very private choice. Others never need to know what something symbolizes to you unless you choose to tell them. Because it's such a private decision, you may not get the chance to know what kinds of items others use to symbolize their important decisions, so we have compiled a list for you. It will not only help you get a full grasp of what we mean by symbols, it may inspire you with ideas to use in selecting your own symbols.

Stand-In Symbols

Stand-In Treasure	Symbol Selected to Represent the Treasure	Significance of the Symbol
Grandfather	Photograph of grandfather	Loved his grandpa deeply
Son	Photograph of son	Treasures her son

Dog	Stuffed animal named "Willie"	"Willie" was a favorite childhood pet
Mother	Lock of mother's hair	Brushing mother's hair was a special, intimate expression of care
Father	Dad's wedding ring worn on a gold chain	Dad took good care of his kids
Friend	Thin gold band on little finger	Wants the best for her friend

How will you symbolize your treasuredness?

Reminding Yourself

- You treasure yourself by getting to know and like yourself.

- Everyone shares a universal need for self-forgiveness.

- Learning to like yourself includes cutting yourself loose from the shame and guilt of past mistakes by forgiving yourself.

- Renewing a positive relationship with yourself will open you up to a new level of positive experiences and relationships.

- If you have lost trust in yourself, it's important to rebuild it through small, intentional steps.

- Making friends with your whole self is vital to living a whole life.

11

Embracing Your Purpose, Mission, and Abilities

As you develop a sense of treasuredness toward yourself, you will naturally want to treasure all parts of yourself, including your purpose, mission, and abilities. No, *especially these*. It's not unusual for people to live and not truly identify their purpose in life. Most people are at least partially living it out, because purpose is simply expressing who you truly are. Missions are another thing, though. Many people miss theirs. It is too easy to let life just happen to you, to be swept along by circumstances and become a *reaction* to life rather than an *initiator* of it. Putting one foot in front of the other wondering what on earth you are really about but not exerting the effort to figure out is all too common.

Many people are unsatisfied living a life that isn't expressing their purpose, their mission, and their unique abilities. It's important for you to know the answers to who you are and what you want to do about it. You need to know. The people close to you need you to know. Your community needs you to know.

The world needs you to know. Imagine a planet where people know themselves, live from their strength, love from their heart, and serve from their passion. There really isn't a logical argument against this, and the experience of it is irrefutable.

Another reason to know the answers to these life questions is so you can set boundaries to protect them from being ignored, misused, and abused. Your purpose, mission, and abilities are among your most valuable goods. Others can see them when you can't, and can take advantage of you if you are not protecting yourself with boundaries. Boundaries are essential. By not identifying your array of personal treasures, or not taking them seriously, you lose the joy and fun of owning and caring for something very special that only you possess.

Identifying Your Purpose

Your purpose is that thing you can't help doing. It's built-in, and can usually be described in three words or less. Purpose is that thing you do that leaves you feeling most competent, alive, and hungry for more. It is the foundation upon which you build your mission and from which you devote consuming, often passionate, attention to a people, task, project, service, or goal.

Discovering Your Purpose

Do you know your purpose? There are several ways to identify it. Here are three:

1. Observe your life, past and present. What is the common, golden thread that runs underneath your most satisfying work and experiences?

2. Ask special people what the two most beautiful things they receive from you are.

3. Ask yourself in what three ways would you love to contribute to the good of others?

Look for a common theme in your answers. To help you fully grasp what purpose is, we offer you this list. Read it through, noting words that match or closely match who you think you are and what you think you do. If you don't find a purpose word on this list, let the list lead you to others.

Purpose Words

Encourager	Healer	Teacher
Mentor	Researcher	Inspirer
Organizer	Creator	Artist
Musician	Calculator	Monitor
Administrator	Helper	Developer
Initiator	Director	Designer
Server	Problem-Solver	Caretaker
Doer	Manager	Builder
Broker	Discoverer	Engineer
Dreamer	Performer	Entertainer
Comedian	Craftsman	Cleaner
Culinarian	Protector	Distributor
Advocate	Architect	Grower
Beautifier	Restorer	Fixer
Seller	Driver	Warehouseman
Provider	Benefactor	Communicator
Planner	Trainer	Forecaster
Scholar	Coordinator	Systemizer

Discovering your purpose is a very private journey, but this doesn't mean it has to be a lonely one. The people who love and respect you can help you see yourself more accurately than you do on your own, and can confirm conclusions you draw.

Owning Your Purpose

Which word on the purpose word list, if any, struck a knowing chord within you? Perhaps more than one seems to describe you. Keep them both. Adjust them later, if necessary.

Please write a few of your purpose words here:

I am a(n) _____

Date: _____

You will use this again in the next section.

Treasuring Your Purpose

You will treasure your purpose when you develop and display it in meaningful ways. Some people fear that once they have identified their purpose, they will be compelled to make dramatic life changes that could turn their world upside down. This is a misconception of what purpose is. Because your purpose is who you most are, it will go with you wherever you are and whatever you are doing. For example, if the purpose word you chose is "manager," you will be at your best and most passionate self when you are managing: managing money, managing a party, managing a move, managing accounts, managing care for your aging parent, managing a walk-a-thon, or managing meetings. You are who you are and you get to be that, because being something or someone you are not has never worked for anyone.

Purpose is simply living out who you are in the context of what you already do or may choose to do in the future. Sometimes the dreams or mission that occur as you live out your purpose require you to make changes. In the meantime, treasure your purpose by taking it seriously, by protecting and preserving it with effective boundaries so you can present it in its finest form.

How is your purpose showing in your life now?

In relationships: _____

_____

_____

At home: _____

_____

_____

At work: _____

_____

_____

In hobbies: _____

_____

_____

Identifying and Treasuring Your Mission

Your mission is your purpose in action. It is the expression your purpose takes at a given time. It is the fire your purpose lights when you see something that excites, ignites, or disturbs you. For example, imagine you are a twenty-three-year-old man, a "born teacher" in your first year of teaching first grade. Your teaching experience exposed you to the enormous literacy gap among children. The awareness ignited a mission within you to teach each child in your class to read. You are passionate about it. You gather reading tools for various learning styles, you conduct parent workshops to help parents learn how to help their kids read at home, you attend continuing education classes to improve your own skills, and you make instruction interesting to readers at all levels. Your mission is "teach first graders to read."

In your thirties, you get passionate about teaching teachers how to help kids read. Your purpose is still to teach. Your mission has been re-formed to "helping kids read by training their teachers." In your forties, you get excited about an idea you have developed to teach language, and you've also been wanting to live outside the United States. So, your mission becomes teaching English as a second language in Germany using innovative methods. In your fifties, you join forces with a friend and open the Community Reading Lab where people of all ages can learn to read, and where reading specialists are trained. Your mission is to end illiteracy by teaching people of all ages to read, and training teachers and parents to help kids read. Your purpose didn't change, but your mission took different forms as one opportunity or idea led to another.

Kate's purpose is "creator." Kate is most satisfied and successful when her mission fulfills her purpose. In her teens, before Kate even thought of identifying herself as creative, she successfully led a local campaign to allow young artists to paint murals along community alleyways. She married in her sophomore year of college, took a full-time job with the state for a year, then became pregnant with the first of two children. She chose happily to stay home with her kids until the youngest was in kindergarten. With the new free time on her hands, she began to ask the question, "What now?" A friend suggested she take seriously her natural inclination to create beauty in whatever situation, project, or location she was in. Kate had never consciously realized that's

what she did, yet when her friend mentioned it, Kate acknowledged that it was true. In college, she had transformed a drab
dorm room into a lively, happy environment. Her wedding was
filled with beauty, from the invitations, to the decorations, to the
programs, to the thank you notes. Her home, run-down when
they bought it, was now a warm and beautiful dwelling inside
and out, a direct result of Kate's drive to make beauty. Friends
frequently asked Kate to help them decorate their homes and
coordinate accessories. But she saw it as a hobby, not a purpose
or passion, until her friend's remark that day. So, she explored
opportunities in interior design, and for several years she was an
indispensable assistant to a respected designer in her town. In
the course of doing this work, as so often happens, another mission, a different expression of her purpose, presented itself to
Kate. It resembled her high school mural effort and rekindled
Kate's passion for making a city a more beautiful place to live.
She became director of an urban beautification project, living out
her purpose through a new mission.

Depending on her talents, Kate could have expressed her
purpose of creating toward a number of missions: beautifying
faces, hair, bodies, schools, shelters, hospital rooms, wardrobes,
gardens, waterways, boring walls, old furniture, lives, moments,
celebrations, or cakes.

What would you go to the wall for? Literacy? Local recycling? Education that honors all learning styles? Credit reports
that are easier to correct? Higher salaries and better training for
geriatric assistants? Like most people, you probably care about
these things, but as a unique individual, what really moves you,
upsets you, or gets under your skin? Or, on the other hand, what
excites you, stimulates you, produces energy within you and makes
you feel like time is running out? What makes you feel competent
and complete? Somewhere within your answer is your mission.

Discovering Your Mission

There are two routes you can take to discover your mission.
One is to look for what issue, cause, field, or service you would
"go to the wall for." What upsets you? Delights you? Fascinates
you? Makes perfect sense to you? Seems only right? Gives you
a thrill? Find that "thing" and then ask, "How can I fulfill my
purpose within it?" For example, Ron is someone who is very
concerned that massive adjustments in global thinking will be

required to save the planet from drying up, winding down, and going under. He wants to devote himself to this cause. He has identified his purpose as "visionary-communicator," meaning he has a special way of seeing the world and communicating what he sees in a way that causes people to listen. Ron can merge his purpose with his mission in a number of ways, depending on his abilities, season of life, and resources.

A second way to discover your mission is to live out your purpose and let your mission find you. In other words, refine the skills that your purpose brings out in you, regardless of how you are expressing it, then stay alert to that certain issue, cause, field, or service that "calls your name." For example, Sandra's purpose is "systemizer." She has a well-trained love and ability to create systems that keep people or projects working smoothly. One day, her supervisor introduced her to a new client, the creative director of a live theatre company. Sandra had a life-long passion for the theatre and had often wished she could work in the field. Later, after observing her excellence, the director offered Sandra a job systemizing costume production and recycling among theatre companies.

Owning Your Mission

You own your mission when you act on it. Acting on a mission takes many forms, from a very small step to altering your life. Ron, the man who wants to adjust global thinking, may choose to own his mission at first by simply increasing his knowledge about global environmental issues. He can read, visit, write, subscribe, search the Internet, initiate dialogue, interview, and travel. Any one of these things will energize him because he is both living out his purpose and his mission. The force of the merge between purpose and mission is a powerful, inspiring sight.

Do you have an idea of what your mission is now?

_____

_____

_____

_____

_____

What other mission options might interest you?

_____

_____

_____

_____

_____

Treasuring Your Mission

You will treasure your mission when you love it and treat it well. Picture yourself finding your mission, loving it, looking for ways to make it come true, and savoring the very thought of it. Imagine if you could put it in your pocket, take it with you, show others who will value it, and spin it round and round in your hand. You would take good care of it, help it grow, and eventually make it happen. This is treasuring your mission.

Identifying Your Abilities

Abilities are the skills you use to carry out your purpose and mission. By abilities, we mean your knowledge, skills, and talents. Knowledge is information you have gathered in your life, skills are those things you have learned to do, and talents are those things you can do naturally and especially well—or could do well if you developed them. It's helpful to imagine your abilities as tools in a toolbox. They are meant to help you complete the jobs and roles you take on in life. The tools in your toolbox are a unique, personalized assortment, and it is imperative to your success that you know what you have and how to use it.

There is a logical way to identify and develop your abilities. It can be summed up in this simple statement: Match your life to your equipment. Would you play serious tennis with a shovel? Would you join a trio without knowing how to harmonize? Would you enter a bike race with a 1954 Schwinn? Equally illogical and unthinkable is having a piece of equipment you need and not using it. Or worse yet, needing it but not knowing you have it. People limit their success, and sense of competence every day by agreeing to things they are not equipped to do, or declining opportunities they are equipped to do but don't have the confidence to accept. They don't play the game of life from the strength of their equipment.

Discovering Your Abilities

How do you identify your abilities? First, you look at what you do well already. Second, you look at what you have done well in the past. And, third, you look inside to see what's in there you haven't developed yet. We often help clients identify what's in their toolbox. Once the tools are identified, we help them sort out what they know how to do from what they like to do. This is important, because there are many things we learn to do that we don't enjoy doing. Optimally, you want to enjoy what you also do well.

What do you do well naturally? (Talk at parties, give speeches, organize events, make people laugh, play music, sympathize, initiate change, think up ideas, bake delicate pastries.)

_____

_____

_____

_____

_____

What skills have you learned? (Sew, hike, give CPR, paint a house, keep books on a computer, direct projects, assist leaders, snowboard, grow orchids, speak French.)

_____

_____

_____

_____

_____

What subjects do you know well enough to intelligently discuss? (Politics, biology, art, preserving foods, rocks, composting, foreign trade, theatre.)

_____

_____

What have you done so far in your life that has felt successful and made you feel competent? (Won a carving contest in fourth grade, successfully endured a solo wilderness trip, directed a cancer-prevention walkathon, pulled our family's history together, lovingly cared for an aging parent.)

Owning Your Abilities

Now, look over your list. These are the abilities you own. They are the tools in your toolbox, a life assortment of skills and knowledge that is yours and yours alone. Keep adding to the list on this page or another, or simply in your mind. But stay aware of the skills you have and the new ones you will receive as your life continues. Appreciate and cultivate them whenever you can.

Treasuring Your Abilities

Next, go back to your list and place a mark by the abilities you own that you particularly treasure, those abilities that you relish using. While you may enjoy many of them, you will probably truly treasure only one or two. This is important information for you to know, because you will want to use what you treasure most. What can you do to treasure your abilities?

- Take them seriously.

- Develop them.

- Use them.

- Enjoy them.

- Protect them.

- Preserve them.

- Present them.

Merging All Three with Your Circumstances, Season of Life, and Resources

There are other influences on how you will express your purpose, mission, and abilities. Your season of life and resources will shape the outcome. These are the elements that make your story unique. Money, responsibilities, health, limitations, challenges, opportunities, windfalls, hardship, acquaintances, and surprises along the way draw their own lines around your purpose, mission, and abilities. Within the circumstances, your season of life, and resources, you get to live out who you are and what you care about using the abilities you have.

Here's a story of Mike, a client. What Mike wanted was to choose a career that matched what he most loved to do. Of course, he wasn't sure what that was at first. Part of the process of self-discovery is awareness, and Mike became aware of something he has done his entire life: he watched and admired spiders. They fascinated him. For years, he had been standing on his deck with a flashlight at night watching the spiders. One day, he realized he would love to play with, talk, and teach about spiders. At the time, he was in a master's program for elementary school teachers, but he felt unsettled about it because within himself he knew he was not cut out for the classroom, especially the elementary level classroom. To his credit, he paid attention to his own voice, and discontinued his program.

Mike's profile revealed that his purpose was, indeed, "teacher." His temperament and other preferences proved his hunch about the elementary level and being inside a classroom every day was correct—he wasn't suited for it. What he did have was an appetite for learning, an ability to feel comfortable alone or with people, and a strong admiration for experts in a field. He is now exploring entomology, with a focus on arachnids. He is reading, interviewing, and experimenting, to discover what part he wants to play. Mike's mission, he has happily discovered, is to learn and study spiders. The form his purpose takes is yet to be identified, but whether or not he carries out his purpose as a professor, a researcher, a writer, or a field guide, Mike will be happy because what he loves will be what he does.

Here is a chart to illustrate the many ways season of life and circumstances influence the expression of a person's purpose and mission:

Purpose and Mission	How it is being expressed in the season of life
Restorer: Make things work again	Mobile fix-it shop
Protector: Help women define and achieve economic security	Financial planner for women
Artist-Grower: Create beautiful environments	Intimate garden designer
Communicator: Keep history alive for children	Writes children's books
Healer: Encourage hurting people	Writes about 100 notes a week to people she knows or knows of
Organizer: Bring order to homes	Organizes closets
Coordinator: Honor special life moments	Writes a "Creative Moments" newsletter and leads seminars
Comedian: Make people laugh	Host of weekly comedy classics for families at local town hall
Protector: Protect people from danger	Director of citizen foot patrol
Grower: Plant flowers everywhere	Operates a 10-acre U-Cut flower and vegetable field
Problem-solver: Create peace through problem-solving	Works with a creative problem-solving organization that consults companies

Your Identity Statement

Most people find it helpful to create a personal identity statement at various stages of their lives. It does several things for you. First, it describes your purpose and mission. Second, it serves as a filter to help you make life decisions. Third, it gives you a checkpoint to evaluate your own evolution as a person. And fourth, it gives you a starting place to clearly describe yourself to employers, friends, and others who ask you to, "Tell me about yourself."

During a seminar, a man was asked to describe himself. He answered, uncomfortably, "I don't know. I'm just a guy." A woman was asked the same question at another table. She tried a little harder to give an answer and said, "I'm a mother of four. Oh, and I sell Avon." When the seminar concluded, we asked the same two people the same question. Their answers had changed remarkably. The man said, "I am a craftsman who loves books and builds beautiful custom cases to hold them." The mother and Avon representative said, "I am a provider who loves to supply people with what they need, including my kids who need me at home, so I sell Avon in my neighborhood."

What changed in these two people? The way they viewed themselves. This was a result of learning who they were and what their purpose was. It was an outcome of treasuring themselves and what they do. If we were to ask you to tell us about yourself, what would your answer be? Would it be different than the description you might have given us at the beginning of the book? Different than it would have been two years ago? Five years ago? Twenty years ago?

Creating Your Identity Statement

Your identity statement can be structured in any way you choose. The important thing is that it clearly state who and what you are today. The following example of an identity statement illustrates how an identity statement can be created no matter where you are in the process of discovery, treasuring, and boundary setting.

- I am a person discovering my purpose and mission and learning to set better boundaries.

- I am a(n) _____ (your purpose word(s)) who is in the process of identifying my mission.

- I am a(n) _____ (your purpose word(s)) with a mission to _____ (your mission).

- I am using my key abilities of _____ to express my purpose as a(n) _____ on a mission to _____ .

Like the stone tossed into a pool causes ripples, so is every adjustment you make to your life. Other things must shift, make room, respond. Making choices is one of those things. It is one last stop before moving on to better boundaries.

You are a treasure. Do you know it?

Reminding Yourself

- It's important to take the time to think about what you're purpose is.

- Your mission expresses your true purpose.

- Realizing your purpose and mission can lead to a more fulfilled and aware lifestyle, and can eventually help you clarify your identity.

12

Making Good Choices

Developing a system to help you make choices that are good for you is a treasuring thing to do as owner of your life. What does it mean to make choices for your own good? It means that your decisions will enhance you, not diminish you. When you're making decisions about where to set your boundaries, you will want to have a system for making choices that works for you.

Making choices is a process of sorting options and setting priorities. It's similar to cleaning your closet. Suppose you have decided to rid your wardrobe of garments you don't enjoy wearing. You open your closet door and begin making decisions about what to toss. You prioritize by keeping only what you want and need. If you have twelve sweaters, but only really like seven of them, you choose those seven, and give the other five to charity. Once the job is done, you stand in front of your closet and experience a high that comes with aligning your choices to your true preferences. This is congruence, and congruence occurs when your lifestyle is an expression of you listening to your Self. As a result, you will experience a sense of confidence and peace. Boundaries allow you to choose what you really want and ignore any input from others telling you your decision was impractical.

Sorting options and setting priorities can be challenging, but as your own best friend you will want to work to figure them out. Author and speaker, Dr. Jerry Canning, recalls making a choice without sorting his options and setting priorities. He and his wife were at a club dancing to the music of one of their favorite entertainers. Jerry was an amateur guitar player taking lessons to get better at it, and he had mentioned this casually when he had struck up a conversation with the leader of the band. Jerry would fantasize about being on stage and playing the guitar. So, when the entertainer, from the stage, invited Jerry to "Come up on stage and play guitar with us," he jumped at the chance. He did not pause to sort through his options—he could have chosen the option of going on stage at a time when he was better prepared. Once in front of the crowd reality dawned on him and he realized he hadn't yet mastered all of the chords and the ones he did know could still sound pretty bad. There, on stage in front of everyone, Jerry realized he had made a bad choice. He changed his mind, went back to his seat, and made plans on a napkin that would lead him in smaller steps to play his guitar on stage someday.

The Stop-Look-Listen System

An effective and easy choice-making system is "Stop-Look-Listen." When you are faced with a choice, you stop before moving ahead, look over the situation, and listen—to yourself, to your intuition, to the wisdom of trusted advisors, or to what your experience has taught you.

Stop. Stop right before you make a choice. If you are at the store deciding whether or not to overspend, on the phone deciding what date is best for a family reunion, or at work debating an offer to take on a new project even though you haven't finished the last one, stop long enough to clear your head and review your options.

Look. Look at the situation from more than one perspective. Ask the following questions:

- What is my motive for making this choice?
- Will it hurt me?
- Will it hurt others?
- Would I choose this option for someone I love?
- Can I change my mind? If not, am I sure I want to make a final decision right now?

- What would the people I trust suggest I do?

Listen. In your mind, try to "hear" these tips from people who have become experts at making choices.

- Listen to your gut, is it telling you that you're being pressured into saying "yes"?

- If someone is pressuring you, remove yourself from the situation.

- Don't make an important decision when you're desperate.

- "Let me think about it" are five words to speak often. Things usually look different the next morning—either better or worse.

Visualizing the future is another effective tool for making choices. Catherine remembers buying a sofa and realizing the next day, as it sat in her living room, that she bought it because she wanted some excitement in her life. Looking at the sofa the following day, Catherine understood that she was expecting the sofa to do for her what she could only do for herself. She still felt that she lacked excitement in her life even after she bought the sofa, and she regretted the purchase. Now, when faced with a similar decision, she asks herself, "Is there a hidden reason for this purchase?" She imagines the future and decides which statement will be likely to make her feel the best, either, "I bought the item," or "I didn't buy the item." Then she makes her choice accordingly. If the morning comes and she regrets not buying something, she can always return to the store at that time.

Treasuring yourself includes developing a way to protect yourself from people, things, and circumstances that aren't in your best interest. Every day you are faced with choices. Your response to them will depend on (1) how highly you treasure yourself, (2) how firmly you believe you are the owner of your life, and (3) how well you use a choice-making system that you have created to make your final decisions.

Choosing to Treasure Yourself

The greatest choice you can make is to be your own best friend. It is from this place of treasuredness you can confidently take yourself to life situations requiring effective boundaries. How friendly do you feel toward yourself? Friendly enough to set better boundaries? It's up to you. You own your life. A client of ours, Karen, chose to treasure herself by making a choice that prompted her to create an effective boundary that benefited both her family and her.

Karen is a woman in her early forties who had to make a hard choice a few years ago. She is married and is the mother of three children. The oldest two left for college within a two-year time span, while the youngest was just starting high school. Karen's husband works for the post office where he has worked for the past fifteen years. Karen never finished her college degree; she had to drop out toward the end of her pregnancy with her oldest child. She always regretted not finishing her education— she had been pursuing a degree in Spanish at the local university.

Although her family insisted that they completely supported the idea of her going back to school, she still felt reluctant. Internal resistors were going off like activated fire alarms in her mind—she had compiled a set of false beliefs about herself after dropping out of college. Her immature defense mechanism caused her to insist that school wasn't really all *that* important, that she had learned enough through staying home and raising a family. However, deep down inside, her intuition was telling her that finishing her degree would be good for her. There were secret fears lurking behind every step she made toward finding out about the continuing education programs. She feared she couldn't do it anymore, that she wouldn't have the energy to stick with all of the work. There was also a lot of guilt surfacing—she felt guilty about "abandoning" her family. She wasn't used to making decisions that seemed to only benefit her, and not her family.

With the help of her family's persistence and support, Karen finally decided to sort through her options. She realized she could just stay home and never finish her degree, or she could enter the program and go at her own speed. Karen chose to listen to her intuition and do what she knew would be difficult, but would eventually be rewarding. She began to look forward to using her mind in a challenging way that she had enjoyed when she was in school twenty years before. The boundary Karen needed to set was between her and her own resistance.

Choosing to go back to school and finish her degree turned out to be one of the best decisions Karen felt she ever made. The decision not only benefited her, but also her family. Karen felt more confidence having overcome a major fear, and her new sense of personal strength gave her the courage to try more things. She got a job working for the city as a translator, which doubled the household income.

Reminding Yourself

- Making good choices is an important part of treasuring yourself.

- The "stop-look-listen" system is a helpful safeguard to keep you from poor choices.

- The greatest choice you can make is to be your own best friend.

- It is from the place of being your own best friend that you can confidently go to life situations requiring effective boundaries.

Part III

Better Boundaries

13

Taking Boundaries to Life Situations

You now know the basics of boundaries and are aware of the importance and process of ownership and treasuredness. It's time, then, to merge them into creating better boundaries. The following examples of life situations will show you how treasuredness and ownership create better boundaries. The boundaries challenges we have featured are in the following areas of life:

Beliefs	Possessions
Body	Relationships
Feelings	Service/Career
Future	Sexuality
Lifestyle	Space
Love	Spirit
Money	Time
	Values

Before moving on to the situations themselves, we want to furnish you with the following clarifiers to help you gain the most benefit from the examples you will be studying:

- The boundary options selected in the situations are not meant to be exhaustive. That would be impossible.

- We encourage you to add options of your own based on your own values, opinions, and experiences.

- The boundary options used in these situations have all passed a test we designed called an "Okay Test." This means they are safe, legal, respectful, and life-enhancing.

- We define "let in the good" as positive, life-building events and "keep out the bad" as negative, life-diminishing events. Your definitions and our definitions may not be the same. This will simply give you a chance to create your own solutions that fit your beliefs and values.

- As you read the situations, note how predicting and evaluating boundary choices ahead of time can increase the success of your choices. This is a good pattern to adopt in your life. Look ahead at what pain, trouble, or loss you will experience if you don't set a boundary in a certain situation, and what gains you will experience if you do.

- When you reach the "My treasured self boundary option" in each situation, please understand the process of creating options. When you're sorting through the options of a situation in your life, start with an "anything goes" empty slate. Come up with an option even if you'd never in your life do it. Then once you have listed the uncensored options, from the ridiculous to the wise, refine the list by filtering the options through a filter that represents your values; it's like creating your own version of an "Okay Test." This process will help you vent your wild possibilities, probably discover some alternatives you wouldn't have thought of if you had censored your options right away, and then come up with some more realistic options to consider.

- The situations feature both internal and external threats to your boundaries. Internal threats, again, are your internal resistors—your false beliefs, thinking errors, and defense mechanisms. External threats are people, situations, and activities.

- As you read the situations, become familiar with the boundary language and behaviors of a treasured self.

- The situations will increase your awareness of the wide variety of daily threats to your boundaries. We suggest you keep your eyes open to other situations that are everywhere, in life, in the media, in movies, and in music. Become a "boundary watcher."

- Let the situations help you grow in confidence and give you the courage to set boundaries in your own life.

- Use the following examples of situations to demystify the work of setting and managing better boundaries.

Beliefs

You have a right to your own set of beliefs, so don't miss out on forming them, speaking them, and setting boundaries with people who infringe on your beliefs. They are critical to your emotional and behavioral well-being, and if you don't exercise respectful ownership of your beliefs, you may find yourself living out the adage, "If you don't stand for something, you'll fall for anything." Set boundaries between your beliefs and anything or particularly anyone who would keep you from owning them.

We want to remind you that everyone has periodic thinking errors that can be problematic in your life and require quick remedies. It's the *patterns* of thinking errors and defense mechanisms that are the most dangerous and require concentrated attention to create the boundaries you want.

Beliefs 1

Who's involved: Self and co-workers.

Situation analysis: I work at a place where the guys are always telling jokes. Lately, I've been feeling uncomfortable about the kinds of jokes being told at work—they're getting pretty raunchy and racist.

The "bad" that may happen if I don't set a boundary: Unrelenting assault on my beliefs that racism and sexism are unacceptable—a sense of not standing up against what I know is wrong.

The "good" I can gain by setting a boundary: Self-respect.

My "treasured self" boundary options:

- Speak out, "I'm feeling pretty uncomfortable with the nature of the jokes."
- Social engineering options—avoid the joke-telling sessions or the jokers when things become uncomfortable.
- Set the tone through countering—model new preferred behavior by telling good jokes that aren't offensive in nature.

Beliefs 2

Who's involved: Self and friends.

Situation analysis: I've been a member of a biker group on the east coast for the last fifteen years. The code that we've lived by has been based on power and control. I liked and respected that kind of life, but recently my wife was in an accident and not expected to live. I never felt so powerless and out of control. I hated it. As I was sitting there in the ER, I remembered one of grandmother's sayings, "When all else fails, pray." In desperation, I did, and my wife improved. I don't know what it all means, but I'm beginning to believe that there is a Power out there that I never considered before. My friends think I'm full of it, and getting weak.

The "bad" that may happen if I don't set a boundary: Continuation of keeping people in my life who do not respect my decision to enrich my life in new ways. By remaining in this situation, I am not able to present my true self.

The "good" I can gain by setting a boundary: Spiritual exploration and growth.

My "treasured self" boundary options:

- Internally challenge the thinking error of *labeling* (for example, the label my friends gave me, "You're *weak* if you can't make it on your own and need to believe in some made-up religious thing").

- Speak out by stating, "I'm not saying I know exactly what I believe is out there, I just know I'm smart enough to pay attention to my gut."

- Maintain a questioning attitude about spiritual possibilities; befriend others who have similar questions.

Body

Treasuring your body by respecting, accepting, and taking care of it is critical if you are to establish and honor boundaries related to it. Honoring your body is based on far more than following and pursuing the culturally driven beauty myths presented by marketing icons. Establishing boundaries between your body and others' critical influence or physical violation is crucial. You also treasure your body by considering what you will put in it, put on it, or what you do to condition it, maintain it, and share it. Finally, what will you allow yourself to think about it?

Body 1

Who's involved: Self, husband, newborn baby, and my parents.

Situation analysis: I've just had a baby and my parents are flying into town for a visit. My concern is that both of my parents are heavy smokers who I used to let smoke inside our house. I've become more health conscious and don't want myself or my family exposed to the smoke. We've made our home a "no smoking zone."

The "bad" that may happen if I don't set a boundary: Harm to our baby's lungs and to ours.

The "good" I can gain by setting a boundary: Clean healthy air, for me, my husband, and our baby, and a new standard of behavior for smokers in our home that matches our values.

My "treasured self" boundary options:

- Stepping over the feeling of fear, and calling my parents to let them know about the "no smoking zone" before they set out for their visit.

- Waiting until my parents come to tell them about the new "no smoking" expectation, thinking maybe it's better to set my boundary in person.

- Making arrangements for my parents to stay at a nearby motel during their visit.

- Arranging for most of the visiting and play time to be outdoors or in a well-ventilated area.

Body 2

Who's involved: Self and man from the recovery group.

Situation analysis: I've been clean and sober for about eight months now. I've been attending an NA group during that time and it's really helped me; but there's a problem. There's this guy at the meeting who always wants to hug me—I mean really mash me. I don't want to start over with another group, but this guy is really getting to me.

The "bad" that may happen if I don't set a boundary: I'll continue to be "mashed" or touched by him physically, and I'll dread coming to group or will invent reasons to avoid him.

The "good" I can gain by setting a boundary: Honest expression of feelings, no more feeling that my body is being touched by someone I feel uncomfortable about.

My "treasured self" boundary options:

- Speak out by telling the guy, "I appreciate your support for my ongoing recovery, but I'm not comfortable with the hugging stuff. I'd appreciate it if you'd give me some physical space—refrain from the hugs."

- Consider environmental engineering, "I really like this group, but it might be a good idea for me to check out some other recovery groups."

- Counter with an alternative behavior. For example, when the man approaches me for the typical hug, I can extend my hand for a handshake. (This might also be the opening for me to tell him that I'd like more space.)

Body 3

Who's involved: Self with friends.

Situation analysis: I was over at friend's house for dinner and I had enough of the rich, tasty food to be comfortable and satisfied. I have been feeling pretty good about myself because lately I've been eating healthy, low-fat food, and I've been eating until I'm content, not stuffed. This time my friend kept pushing me to eat more food. She even began to put more food on my plate.

The "bad" that may happen if I don't set a boundary: My choice to honor what's best for my body will be dismissed, posing a threat to the momentum of my new pattern.

The "good" I can gain by setting a boundary: Establish myself as the one who decides, increase my personal power, maintain and perhaps increase momentum for change.

My "treasured self" boundary options:

- Speak up by saying, "Thank you, but I've had plenty." Leave the food on the plate.

- Take the food, but not actually eat it.

- Use humor to respond to my friend's behavior; say, "I know I won't eat that food so it must be for you."

Feelings

To respond with emotion to the world is to be human. To have your feelings or emotions censored, invalidated, banished, rejected, or ignored is to be sentenced to less than human existence. On the other hand, to emote without consideration for thoughts and behavior is a setup for violating others. So, ownership of your feelings is your right and responsibility. Because people perceive the world differently, your feeling states are uniquely yours to be heard and responded to in a manner that is authentically and respectfully yours. Listen to your feelings, guard them, and manage them for your own good.

Feelings 1

Who's involved: Self and my parents.

Situation analysis: My parents are having a garage sale and they are selling items that I have told them have strong sentimental value to me.

The "bad" that may happen if I don't set a boundary: Jumping to conclusions about their motives, possibility of losing sentimental items. Fractured relationship with my parents, resentment.

The "good" I can gain by setting a boundary: Honest expression of feelings to my parents, perhaps a solution to retaining the items.

My "treasured self" boundary options:

- Consider the possibility that I am using the thinking errors—*mind reading* (e.g., "My parents really don't consider me or my feelings significant") or *emotional reasoning* ("I'm feeling insignificant, I must be insignificant").

- Speak out by reminding my parents that I would like to keep selected items. Be open to the possibility that my parents forgot about my earlier request for the items.

- Take action by making arrangements to pay my parents for the items that I would like to keep. Be open to the possibility that they are embarrassed about needing money.

Feelings 2

Who's involved: Self and dad.

Situation analysis: My precious cat has disappeared. She's been gone for more than a week now and I've been really sad. When my dad sees or hears me crying, he tells me to "Buck up," and, "Get a grip. It was just a stupid cat!"

The "bad" that may happen if I don't set a boundary: Sense of shame over honest grief and loss, resentment toward Dad, accepting discounting of my values.

The "good" I can gain by setting a boundary: Honesty with Dad, new confidence in standing up for my feelings, freedom to grieve without shame, withstand parental belief I don't endorse.

My "treasured self" boundary options:

- Challenge the thinking errors of "should" statements and *intellectualizing*, i.e., "You shouldn't feel ..." or "Don't feel, think your way through this."

- Speak out by saying, "Dad, I know you don't feel the way I do about the cat. I'm not asking you to. What I would like from you is to accept me, and let me grieve in my way. Sadness is not a crime."

Future

Protecting your future means making certain what you're going to experience is, to the best of your ability, positive. For example, if you're committed to living fully in the present moment, but find yourself getting overwhelmed by promises you made but can't keep, you haven't been your own best friend in the way you planned your future. In other words, the future you created was not a pleasant experience to live through. Setting boundaries around your future involves treasuring yourself enough to consciously plan ahead for your own good. This may mean charting a course of goals that will help you live a certain way, or it may mean improving your pattern of overextending yourself and underdelivering so you can look forward to what's ahead.

Future 1

Who's involved: Self and parents.

Situation analysis: I just got my college degree and I planned to take a position overseas with the Peace Corps for the next eighteen months. My parents are against my decision to join the Peace Corps and are now threatening to withdraw their financial assistance that was to help pay off my student loans. They say my decision is irresponsible.

The "bad" that may happen if I don't set a boundary: Give up control of my life to my parents, harbor resentment, feeling of being held hostage by my parents' money.

The "good" I can gain by setting a boundary: Set a new era of relationship as owner of my life, personal responsibility as an adult, honest discussion with my parents, live out the future I feel will be best for me.

My "treasured self" boundary options:

- Speak out by telling them, "Mom, Dad, I love you and would appreciate your financial assistance with my student loans. My decision to go into the Peace Corps is motivated by my worldview and personal values that call me to help other people wherever I can."

- Insist, "Mom, Dad, a short time overseas with the Peace Corps will be an opportunity for me to take global responsibility. While I would appreciate your financial help, if you decide not to help me, I would appreciate knowing that as soon as possible so that I can make other arrangements."

- Speak out, "I'd like to ask you to take a closer look at the Peace Corps with me. In fact, would you go to a meeting with me?"

Future 2

Who's involved: Self and boss.

Situation analysis: The company I've worked for the past eight years doesn't have any advancement opportunity for me, so I've decided to take a few classes to enhance my skills and take a job with another company. My current boss is really angry with my decision. He says I'm putting him in a real bad situation. He even told me that he wouldn't give me a positive employment recommendation if I left.

The "bad" that may happen if I don't set a boundary: Remaining stuck in an unhappy, defeating environment, missed opportunity for personal growth, loss of self-respect and ownership.

The "good" I can gain by setting a boundary: Personal and professional development, confidence in ability to take control of my life, creating new, more positive opportunities.

My "treasured self" boundary options:

- Internally challenge the false guilt and emotional reasoning thinking error. My employer may be in a bad situation, but I didn't put him there, nor am I responsible for finding him a solution.

- Speak out, "While I would appreciate a positive work evaluation from you, I'm committed to my personal and professional development and will be leaving at the end of my two weeks."

- Speak out, "My job performance here is excellent, you have no right to threaten me simply because I am taking classes on my time outside of work to improve the opportunities in my future."

Lifestyle

Show us a person who's trying to live out someone else's lifestyle dream, and we will show you a person who has limited joy and satisfaction. When you get tired of performing to meet other people's expectations, a window of opportunity is being opened to you. Until you've said "enough" to a lifestyle that isn't serving your long-term good as a loving, authentic person, you won't be available to present yourself in the world as who you genuinely are. An authentic lifestyle is a treasured lifestyle.

Lifestyle 1

Who's involved: Self and friends from work.

Situation analysis: The people I work with tend to gather at a pub and drink together after work. I like the idea of hanging out with them socially, but there is usually heavy drinking involved. I'm just not into getting drunk regularly—especially since the last time I ended up getting caught drinking and driving.

The "bad" that may happen if I don't set a boundary: Will probably get drunk, put myself and others in danger by driving, may be arrested, violate my better judgment, and give up control, engage in a lifestyle that isn't in my best interest.

The "good" I can gain by setting a boundary: Celebration with friends from work and a chance to enjoy these work relationships without complications.

My "treasured self" boundary options:

- Speak up and tell the group, "I'm glad to socialize with you for a while—I've got to go in an hour or so."

- Take action by making plans to leave my car at home, and prearrange for someone to pick me up at a certain time.

- Social engineering—refuse all offers for a ride home with anyone who is intoxicated.

- Social engineering—make arrangements to hang out with someone from work who has the same goal (to celebrate without getting intoxicated).

- Make a decision to keep the socializing at the pub to a minimum—for example, agree to go out only on Wednesday nights for a drink.

Lifestyle 2

Who's involved: Self, kids, neighbor, and a dog.

Situation analysis: The neighbors next door have a vicious dog that is digging his way under the fence into our back-yard. I'm afraid for my kids' safety in our yard. I want to have a backyard environment that is both fun and relaxing.

The "bad" that may happen if I don't set a boundary: Challenge to my peaceful lifestyle, fear that the dangerous dog will hurt my kids, damage to my property, eroding relationship with my neighbor.

The "good" I can gain by setting a boundary: Safety for my kids, honesty with neighbor, taking responsibility for my own property.

My "treasured self" boundary options:

- Environmental intervention—strengthen the fence.
- Speak out, "Your dog is a danger to my family and he's destroying the fence. Do whatever you need to do to keep it away from the fence at all times."
- If the problem persists, I will contact animal control officials.

Love

It is possible to arrange a marriage, or arrange to have sex, but you just can't arrange love. As much as others might like to think they know what's best for your love life, the truth is, who and how you will love is your decision. Establishing respectful boundaries between your love for yourself and others is an essential skill that can only be sustained if you hold firmly to the belief of your significance and worth.

Love 1

Who's involved: Self, friends, and family.

Situation analysis: I've been dating this very special person for a while now. He's attractive, interesting, respectful, and very enjoyable to be with. I believe he is a committed to me and it's just a matter of time before he asks me to marry him. Many family members and friends think I'm crazy for thinking of marrying someone eighteen years older than me.

The "bad" that may happen if I don't set a boundary: I will be living and loving for other people, miss out on a loving long-term relationship, give up my right to be owner of my life.

The "good" I can gain by setting a boundary: To love and be loved by another kindhearted human being.

My "treasured self" boundary options:

- Speak out, "I realize you think you know what's in my best interest, but my head and my heart are saying 'yes' to this man whom I've come to love."

- Demand respect for your choices, "All relationships have their challenges, some of ours are easier to see and to plan for."

- Verbally challenge the preconceived judgments of my friends and family, "Why do you believe that a sensitive and caring man doesn't deserve, or isn't entitled to, my love because of his age?"

Love 2

Who's involved: Self and daughter.

Situation analysis: I am a single mother raising my teenage daughter, Rachel. I love her deeply, but it is hard to meet her financial demands. She cannot understand why I won't take her shopping for school clothes at the most expensive and trendy stores. She insists that if I really loved her, I would want her to feel proud and confident about herself with her friends by dressing her in expensive clothes.

The "bad" that may happen if I don't set a boundary: I will create an adult who will have unrealistic expectations of what she is entitled to (materialistically), I will set a pattern of Rachel taking advantage of and not respecting my decisions.

The "good" I can gain by setting a boundary: To be respected by my daughter and still let her know I love her in other ways besides materialistically, raise a woman who understands monetary limitations.

My "treasured self" boundary options:

- Stand firm in my decision to buy Rachel attractive but reasonably priced clothes for school.

- Show my love for Rachel in other nurturing and fun ways.

- Buy her the clothes she really wants on special occasions—birthdays, winter holidays, and so on.

Money

Money is one of those highly charged commodities—we all need it, use it, and invariably, want more of it. So, when you don't have enough, or it's stolen, withheld, threatened, or neglected, someone's going to pay! Setting boundaries around your finances doesn't mean that you should hoard it, hide it, or serve it. Rather, it means that you must learn to set boundaries about how you handle money issues in a manner that is consistent with your values and life mission so you can make your money do what you want it to.

Money 1

Who's involved: Self and friend.

Situation analysis: A friend wants to borrow some money. Actually, he wants to borrow some *more* money—he hasn't repaid (as agreed) the money he borrowed three months ago. I resent my friend for putting me in a situation where I feel like I'm the one who isn't being a good friend if I say "no" to his most recent request.

The "bad" that may happen if I don't set a boundary: Continuing to give up my hard-earned money, putting friendship at risk, anxiety, and perhaps resentment.

The "good" I can gain by setting a boundary: Honesty with a friend, self-control, alignment with my values about loaning/borrowing.

My "treasured self" boundary options:

- I can choose to forgive the debt owed—doing the necessary "letting go" to be at peace internally and externally with my friend.

- Speak out by saying "no."

- Speak out, "I value your friendship. I'm also finding that these money deals are making me feel uncomfortable. I'd rather be your friend than your banker."

Money 2

Who's involved: Self and panhandlers.

Situation analysis: Every day on my way to work I pass a corner where people stand holding a sign that reads, "homeless, hungry, please help, God bless you." I am overcome with guilt if I don't give money, so I have been going the long way to work to avoid them.

The "bad" that may happen if I don't set a boundary: Manipulation, giving out of guilt rather than joy, damaging pattern of avoidance.

The "good" I can gain by setting a boundary: A plan of intentional giving to charity of my real choice, absence of guilt and dread, return to shorter way to work.

My "treasured self" boundary options:

- Celebrate my capacity to see the value of all persons, including those with less, and only give money when I want to.

- Confront the thinking error of *emotional reasoning* (i.e., I feel guilty, therefore I am guilty).

- Social action: Do something about my feelings of guilt by contributing to the common good in a way that is consistent with my values, abilities, and resources by identifying community assistance resource agencies to determine how best to help those in need.

- Pack an extra lunch to give away on my way to work if I decide that is the way I wish to contribute.

Money 3

Who's involved: Self and neighborhood kids.

Situation analysis: School has started and I have kids coming to the door every week to raise money for another activity or club. There is no way I can give to all of them even though I'd like to. It's getting so I don't want to answer the door when I see the kids approaching my house.

The "bad" that may happen if I don't set a boundary: Succumb to internal pressure, put family finances at risk, possible bad feelings in the neighborhood between my kids and friends.

The "good" I can gain by setting a boundary: Less anxiety, creative plan, knowledge that I did my best.

My "treasured self" boundary options:

- Prioritize by establishing a "first come, first serve" rule—the kid who gets to me first, gets the donation.

- Create a budget for community donations, and maybe give one dollar to each of the first ten kids that come to the door.

- Social engineering—create work parties or chores that neighborhood kids can do for cash to be applied to their fund-raisers.

- State my limits, "Sorry kids, I can't help you out this time."

Possessions

Everyone's got stuff. You might have more stuff, or different stuff, or more valuable stuff than your friends, but if you don't establish boundaries between your possessions and other people—including realistic guidelines for how they are to be treated—then your claim is, in effect, null and void. Essentially, your stuff is in the public domain and up for grabs when you don't set firm boundaries. Taking care of your possessions by setting boundaries is self-treasuring behavior.

Possessions 1

Who's involved: Self and roommate Jimmy.

Situation analysis: My roommate won't stay out of my room, he's always in my stuff. He borrows my clothes without my permission, my CDs, my computer, it's endless. He has no concept of the fact that my possessions are the result of my hard work and I don't appreciate his disrespectful treatment of my possessions.

The "bad" that may happen if I don't set a boundary: Anger, suspicion, fear of broken property, fights.

The "good" I can gain by setting a boundary: Security, honest confrontation, clearer understanding, better relationship, mature solution.

My "treasured self" boundary options:

- Speak out by voicing my frustrations, "Hey, Jimmy, I know you think my stuff is cool, but I would like you to respect my privacy and possessions by staying out of my room and my things."

- Emphasize my anger at his lack of consideration, "Jimmy, if I'm in my room and give you permission to come in, that's okay. But it's never okay to borrow my things without asking me if I feel comfortable with you using them. Is that clear?"

- Environmental engineering—install a lock on my door.

Possessions 2

Who's involved: Self and teenage son.

Situation analysis: My son borrowed the car last night, and when I went out to drive to work this morning the gas tank was almost empty.

The "bad" that may happen if I don't set a boundary: I may be late to work, my son will continue to be insensitive to other people's possessions, and I will mistrust and resent his use of my things.

The "good" I can gain by setting a boundary: Honest and loving confrontation, new trust, improved relations and co-operation, I become a positive role model for handling of problems.

My "treasured self" boundary options:

- Voice my reasonable expectations—be firm with my limits. Respectfully tell my son, "A condition for using the car is to return it with at least a half a tank of gas."

- Responsibly safeguard my peace of mind by keeping a full can of gas in the garage.

- Communicate my expectations and what the consequences will be if they are not met. "You may not use the car for two weeks if you return the car with an empty gas tank, unless there is an unavoidable circumstance that you can explain to me."

Relationships

It is in the realm of relationships that boundaries are most often set, challenged, breached, and redefined. Those who have invested the time and energy needed to develop a lifestyle marked with clear, respectful boundaries have enriching and meaningful relationships. That's it. Successful, winsome relationships are bounded by limits motivated by treasuredness.

Relationships 1

Who's involved: Self and boyfriend.

Situation analysis: My boyfriend and I have been living together for a while. It's okay most of the time, but when he drinks things can get pretty scary. He gets mean and calls me some really awful things—in front of my kids and anyone else who might be around.

The "bad" that may happen if I don't set a boundary: Accepting his dehumanizing behavior, physical and emotional abuse, humiliation, pose a risk to me and my kids.

The "good" I can gain by setting a boundary: Safety, self-respect, become a positive role model for my kids.

My "treasured self" boundary options:

- Environmental engineering—Because my children and I are physically or emotionally unsafe, I will leave with careful planning and support.
  (**Important Note:** Most of the worst assaults and murders occur in domestic abuse cases when the victim is planning to leave or has left an abuser. Set clear, **safe** boundaries with the help of a trained victim's advocate.)
- Speak out (when he is sober) by telling him, "I believe I, and my children, are valuable. Your abusive language and behavior indicate that you do not honor me or us. Honor us by changing the behavior now (i.e., drinking, abuse) or living together is not an option."
- Seek support—identify a safe support network who will honor your essence. This could include a domestic violence support group, an Al-Anon group, or community of faith.

Relationships 2

Who's involved: Self, husband, newborn baby, and mother.

Situation analysis: I'm about ready to have my first baby and my husband and I are really excited. I want to share the birthing moment with my husband; however, my mother is also planning to be present.

The "bad" that may happen if I don't set a boundary: Anxiety over what I want to be a very special event, frustration that my mom isn't considering my need to decide who will attend this event with my family, sadness that I could lose the intimacy of the moment between my husband and I.

The "good" I can gain by setting a boundary: Fulfill my choice as an adult to have this birthing experience only include me and my husband, establish adult independence and put my relationship with mom on a new level by stating my needs, and still be her caring daughter.

My "treasured self" boundary options:

- Counter my internal resistor of *fortune telling*—that is, predicting the future with the belief that the birthing event will be ruined, and set my boundary accordingly.

- Declare clearly to mom that, "I would like the actual birth to be an event reserved for me and my husband."

- Let mom know at what level and in what ways I would like her to be involved, "Mom, you're welcome to come to the hospital, but please stay in the waiting area until we invite you into the birthing room," and remind her of the ways I do want her included by offering reading material about being a new grandmother.

Relationships 3

Who's involved: Self and others.

Situation analysis: It always seems like the people around me who are having problems and are out-of-control look to me to make things better. Crisis after crisis, from place to place, job to job, and relationship to relationship, my friends depend on me for around-the-clock advice and comfort. I must have a sign on my back that says "the helper is in." The problem is, I can't say "no" to people in need even when it is terrible timing for me.

The "bad" that may happen if I don't set a boundary: Burnout from giving self away, compulsive serving and pleasing, one-way relationships.

The "good" I can gain by setting a boundary: Personal responsibility and limit setting, time and energy for myself.

My "treasured self" boundary options:

- Confront the thinking error of emotional reasoning ("I feel bad when I say 'no,' so I am bad when I say 'no'").

- Take charge of my setting boundaries in my relationships with my friends by getting the assistance needed to establish the criteria for when to say "yes" and when to say "no." Get help for my own "pleaser crisis" before "helping" others.

- Practice saying "no" to others and "yes" to myself more often.

Service

When you know what your purpose is, enjoy doing it, and do it well, you have identified your personal reservoir of potential from which you can contribute with joy and excellence. When your service and/or career spring from this pool, you and your world are built up and enhanced. If, on the other hand, your service is a duty or a chore—without joy or commitment to excellence, you and the world lose. Setting boundaries that allow you to say "no" to the opportunities that don't fit who you are enables you to be ready, willing, and able to say "yes" to contributions that stem from your purpose.

Service 1

Who's involved: Self and employer.

Situation analysis: I've been working at a local software company for six months, long enough for me to realize that it's not utilizing my talents. I can do the work, I can even do it well, but I hate it.

The "bad" that may happen if I don't set a boundary: Dread the days, become bored, yearn for work that interests me.

The "good" I can gain by setting a boundary: Take charge, make myself available for work I enjoy, invest time and energy into pursuing something more suited to my interests.

My "treasured self" boundary options:

- Speak out and say to my employer, "I can do this work, but I'm finding that it's not a good fit. I'd like to continue working here. Do you have any recommendations for positions that would require more from me in areas that I excel?"

- Take some action by myself, or with the help of a coach or career counselor, and identify what it is that I enjoy doing and do well, then seek a position that fits.

- Continue in my current position but look for ways to be productive outside of my job—ways that will bring me joy as I serve.

Service 2

Who's involved: Self and family.

Situation analysis: I've come from a long line of doctors—my mother, father, grandfather, two uncles, and even my younger sister. I've always been expected to become a doctor, too. I hate the idea of becoming a doctor. I want to become a photojournalist.

The "bad" that may happen if I don't set a boundary: Living out my family's dream, not mine.

The "good" I can gain by setting a boundary: Following my own dream, live passionately, establish my own path.

My "treasured self" boundary options:

- Counter the labeling, I realize that I've been labeled "the odd one" in this family, and yes, I do see myself as quite unique and extraordinary *in this family*. Anyone in this family can become a doctor, the real challenge is to become something else.

- Speak out and tell my family, "My gifts and calling differ from yours. Not better or worse, just different."

- Speak out, "Life's too short to work in a career that doesn't inspire me. Would you want to be operated on by a doctor who hates his job?"

Sex

All boundaries are intended to establish and safeguard your internal and external space to give you room to express your being in a way that's safe and effective. When others, operating from their own set of values and motives, get too close for your comfort sexually, you have a right to set limits. Defining for yourself, and declaring for others, your boundaries regarding sex creates a safe environment for you to thrive, not just survive.

Sex 1

Who's involved: Me and my therapist.

Situation analysis: My husband always seems to be preoccupied with work. When I ask him to take some time to meet my needs, he always has excuses for why he can't. Lately, I've been going to Mark, a therapist, to figure out what to do. It's wonderful to have a man pay attention to me, to listen, and to say all the right things. In just a few weeks, we have become very close. I've especially enjoyed the lingering hug Mark gives me at the end of each session. Last week he surprised, confused, and excited me when he told me he would rather be my lover than my therapist. Tonight my husband is out of town, and Mark wants to "meet my legitimate sexual needs" at a remote hotel.

The "bad" that may happen if I don't set a boundary: Failed attempt to find a healthy resolution to my marriage dilemma; loss of objective therapeutic assistance; entering an intimate sexual relationship with a virtual stranger based on neediness; artificial, and temporary solution.

The "good" I can gain by setting a boundary: Sexual safety and sanity, time to carefully sort through my options.

My "treasured self" boundary options:

- Speak up and firmly say "no" to the invitation.
- Evaluate the situation and recognize my therapist has his own issues.
- Seek input from therapist who is not sexually or relationally motivated.

Sex 2

Who's involved: Self and husband.

Situation analysis: I've had a really long day and I'm not in the mood for sex tonight. The problem is, my husband won't leave me alone so that I can get to sleep. He thinks it's funny, but I'm getting angry.

The "bad" that may happen if I don't set a boundary: Uninspired sex, sense of being used and discounted, growing resentment, loss of needed sleep.

The "good" I can gain from setting a boundary: Rest, honesty, self-respect, choice over my body.

My "treasured self" boundary options:

- Speak out my ownership clearly, "I'm flattered that you want my body, but it's mine to give ... or not, and I'm not giving tonight."

- State assertively, "I'm exhausted. Please respect my 'no.'"

- Counter, "I know you're horny now but I'm exhausted. Lets make love in the morning."

Spirit

Spirit is your sum and substance. It's the core of your being, your essence. To establish boundaries that honor your spirit means that you will not stand for anything or anyone that diminishes your value or rights. When you treasure your spirit, attempts by any-one—even yourself—to discount your value will be rejected out-right. You will know that you are, as the Hebrew psalm declares, "fearfully and wonderfully made." To safeguard your essence is to become a champion for your right to be a meaningful con-tributor in the dynamic existence we call life.

Spirit

Who's involved: Self and community members.

Situation analysis: My skin color causes me to stand out in my neighborhood. As a result, I get a lot of attention—and grief—from some. It's like they suspect me and reject me without even knowing who I am.

The "bad" that may happen if I don't set a boundary: Pos-sible assault to self-esteem, loss of opportunity to freely par-ticipate in neighborhood, continued mistreatment in my area of people who are "different."

The "good" I can gain by setting a boundary: Personal strength to withstand prejudice; self-respect in standing up to injustice; opportunity to demonstrate my courage and heart.

My "treasured self" boundary options:

- Internally counter other's thinking error of *labeling* (i.e., "My skin is a different color than my neighbors. So what! I have a significant contribution to make here by applying myself. I am most certainly not 'shiftless,' or 'lazy.')

- Take action by looking for a way to contribute positively, presenting myself as who I am in the neighborhood.

- Speak out by saying, "I'm glad to have a chance to contribute to the community with my talents. Please let me know where I can help."

- Environmental and social engineering—connect with those in the neighborhood that are respectful and when possible, avoid those who are not.

Time

One of the central units of measure in our society and the world is time. We live by it, press against it, and try to cheat it. Time is precious, and your well-being is directly related to how you choose to use it. If you fail to establish boundaries around your time, chaos and resentment will be your constant companions.

Time 1

Who's involved: Self and wife.

Situation analysis: It's late and I'm really tired, but my wife wants to talk about her frustrations about the kids. I have to wake up early in the morning for work, and if I stay awake to talk I will be useless at work.

The "bad" that may happen if I don't set a boundary: Fatigue and spousal distress, frustration from my wife that I can't meet her needs as a listener and parent.

The "good" I can gain by setting a boundary: Rest and attentive listening at a more appropriate time for me.

My "treasured self" boundary options:

- Communicate my dilemma, "I'm feeling exhausted and really need some sleep or I will be lousy tomorrow."

- Speak out with sensitivity but firmly, "I understand that your are feeling frustrated, I can appreciate how that could be, but I'm so tired I'd prefer to continue the conversation in the morning. Then you can have my alert and undivided attention."

- Compromise, "Is there anything that has to be done tonight? If not, I'll try to listen, but if you hear snoring, it's not because I don't care."

Time 2

Who's involved: Self and a friend.

Situation analysis: A friend has dropped by my office to talk about something that's bugging him. He didn't have an appointment and my day is jammed up with pressing projects and calls to be returned.

The "bad" that may happen if I don't set a boundary: Feelings of frustration, mounting work, resentment, and worry.

The "good" I can gain by setting a boundary: Honest relationship, work would be completed.

My "treasured self" boundary options:

- Speak out and tell my friend, "I'd like to help you sort through this stuff another time. With my schedule so jammed up today, I know I wouldn't be able to give you the attention you deserve. Let's schedule a time to get together ASAP."

- Speak up and tell my friend, "My day's really full, but I can give you five minutes now, and talk more later."

Values

What you value has merit, worth, and significance to you. Your values are your internal guiding, or filtering, principles that help you sort through the millions of options you confront in your lifetime. Your values help you choose the people, beliefs, and activities that will receive your greatest investment, attention, and devotion. It is critical to safeguard your values from manipulation by others because your values so clearly define who you are.

Practicing ownership over your values is a foundation for all other boundary issues. This is where you determine what's okay and not okay for you. And if you don't, others will be there to do it for you.

Values

Who's involved: Self, husband, and teenaged children.

Situation analysis: I want to be with my family in the evenings, but I usually end up having to join them as they watch TV, and become upset by the content of the shows they watch.

The "bad" that may happen if I don't set a boundary: Frustration over violence and pettiness of shows, amount of time spent in front of the television without talking to one another, loss of influence over my children.

The "good" I can gain by setting a boundary: Open, democratic discussion, reestablish communication, model values and the consequences of sticking to them as a parent.

My "treasured self" boundary options:

- Plan of action: I can schedule a family meeting to discuss television issues and alternative choices or schedules.

- Environmental engineering—I can find something else to do in the room during certain shows, like listening to my favorite music on earphones while working a crossword puzzle.

- Speak up and share my concerns with my family, "I know I'm the one in the family who doesn't like the television programming. The thing is, I do like you, my family, and I would like to spend some time together without the distraction of the TV. Can we find a solution?"

- I can negotiate a solution that involves honest and open discussion about the plots of certain programs and alternative outcomes.

Part IV

The Treasured Life

14

Successful Stories

The treasured life is a natural outcome of being your own best friend, owning your life, and setting better boundaries. At some point in the process, you'll discover you have developed patterns of self-care and contribution, you'll find yourself more easily adjusting your flexible boundaries and holding tight to your inflexible ones. You'll become aware of increased calmness within yourself and will experience "breathing room" in your life. You'll realize you are being more intentional about your choices and freer to experiment with what might interest you. Your relationships will undergo adjustments and you will find yourself pursuing friendship with people who are loving, respectful, and inspiring to you. You'll begin expressing your creativity in bolder ways and will find satisfying paths for giving to the common good. And, at some point along the way, you will know you are living the treasured life, not a perfect life, but a treasured one.

What do you think of when you imagine a treasured life? Do you see a mother laughing with her child as they rumble through crunchy fallen leaves in autumn? Do you picture a couple sipping coffee and talking on a couch? Do you imagine a man stopping midday to do deep breathing for three minutes? The treasured life is a composite of many pictures depending on who is living it, but most people who live treasured lives have certain things in common. They simply, for the most part and to the best of their ability, experience a growing pattern of well-being that includes living in the moment, learning new things, expressing their purpose, loving themselves and others more openly, and protecting it all with boundaries that work.

To give you a glimpse of the treasured life, we gathered a small group of men and women together whose lives fit this description. We asked them to talk about how setting new boundaries has increased the quality of their life. Before eavesdropping on their comments, we want to introduce them to you:

Jake is fifty-two, self-employed as a remodeler, and married.

Sandy is fifty, Jake's wife, and works with him in the business.

Ann is thirty-seven, a project manager with a major insurance company, and single.

Larry is forty-eight, in sales, and recently divorced.

Mona is twenty-seven, married, and a stay-at-home mother of two.

Question: How comfortable are you with the idea that you seem to be living the treasured life?

Larry: I always have to get over the idea that the treasured life means a perfect life. Mine's not perfect, not even close.

Sandy: I'm becoming more comfortable with it because I know it doesn't mean I've got it all together. It just means I'm taking good care of myself and my life. I'm okay with that.

Ann: I love it. It's affirming and tells me the work I've done is visible, real.

Question: What have been your challenges to setting effective boundaries in your life?

Mona: I had to get over thinking that boundaries would make me rude. They don't.

Sandy: Me, too. I used to be a pleaser who had few boundaries, so the challenge for me was fear that I would upset people. My fear came true in some cases but I found out upsetting people for healthy reasons is sometimes a good thing.

Jake: The challenge for me was setting boundaries against myself, like overthinking everything. I had always thought of boundaries as being only between people, not between me and my defeating thoughts and habits.

Ann: My challenge was that once I "got it" about boundaries, I wanted to install them everywhere, all at once. Not a good idea. Step-by-step is best.

Larry: I had trouble believing it was really okay to say "no." It's just not a word I said very often to protect myself.

Question: What benefits have you experienced by setting boundaries?

Larry: Freedom.

Ann: Absolutely. And a sense of control and intentionality.

Mona: I think one of the biggest benefits is a growing confidence in the choices I make. Another one is that my life seems simpler.

Sandy: I agree with all of you, plus for me, boundaries have let me concentrate on things I really care about doing, not on things I feel obligated to do.

Jake: Basically, boundaries have brought a sense of calmness to my life. Things are clearer now, not as chaotic.

Question: What has setting boundaries done for your sense of ownership over your life?

Sandy: It has made me feel much more responsible for my life in a very positive way.

Mona: I don't feel at the mercy of others' wishes. I can consider an invitation to a party, for example, weigh whether or not it's in my best interest and the interest of my children for me to go, and then make a good decision based on what I believe rather than on what someone wants me to say.

Jake: Boundaries have definitely increased my sense of ownership. I'm much more inclined to consider options now that I wouldn't have before because I realize more and more that I can choose what to let into my life.

Question: What do you generally keep out of your life now that you used to let in?

Ann: Irritating and boring experiences that aren't required for my job. (Laughter) Seriously, I do my best to spend time with people and things that interest and enrich me. I've become very selective about how I spend my time and with whom.

Larry: I don't let criticism into my life from people I don't respect.

Mona: I keep halfhearted commitments out of my life now. It leaves me more time with the kids, my first commitment, and saves the rest of the time for things I really want in my life. Oh, yes, I keep daytime television out of my life now, too.

Question: What do you let into your life now that you used to keep out?

Sandy: Fun. Just for the fun of it.

Larry: Help from other giving people. I was always the giver. Now I'm also a receiver.

Mona: Education. I'm taking a correspondence course that I wouldn't have considered before because my life seemed out-of-control.

Jake: Coffee breaks with the guys. And I'd say I'm letting in more spirituality.

Ann: Relationships. High quality ones with women and men.

Question: How has setting boundaries increased your care and love of yourself?

Ann: I feel like boundaries have given me my life back. I'm so glad to have it back that I am eager to take good care of it. Kind of like finding something very special you had lost.

Mona: It has increased my value of myself somehow. I rest more, laugh more, get help faster, let myself dream, try new things, and give myself room to be human.

Larry: I'm not nearly as hard on myself as I used to be, not as driven to perform.

Sandy: Because boundaries help me keep my life from becoming overcrowded, I spend more time nurturing myself physically and spiritually.

Jake: I started playing the guitar again. It feeds my soul and makes me happy.

Question: What choices do you make to treasure yourself?

Ann: Hot baths and candles, playing my African drums, books of all kinds, clothes and décor that match my style, new experiences, honest relationships, cards sent to friends and family, visits with my nieces and nephews, wine and conversation with my neighbors, catalog shopping, and donations of time and money at our local domestic violence shelter.

Mona: Massage once a month, once a week visits with two special friends to talk things through and laugh, surprising the kids with fun things to do, journaling, reading my favorite magazines, filling the house with color and music, walks to the park, writing letters to the editor about things that matter to me, and meditating.

Jake: Holding Sandy, playing the guitar, taking pictures of scenes I love, calling my parents and brothers, planning trips, finding additions to my electric train set, sitting on the porch at sunset, taking deep sniffs of good cooking, getting regular medical checkups, mowing our neighbor's lawn—she is a widow.

Sandy: Well I'd better say "holding Jake." I wouldn't be lying either. We love to cuddle and do it more now than ever before. I also mentor a fifth grade boy at a local school, I take classes—anything that interests me, from art to accounting, collect quotes that inspire me, listen to talk radio while I'm working and spout my own opinions about the topic to no one in particular, do Tai Chai, and try to encourage at least one person every day.

Larry: Holding Jake is not on my list, but holding a cold glass of beer at the end of the day is. I also treat myself well by making my daughter's lunch every morning—really special lunches, playing with my dog every day, swimming in the mornings, treating my clients really well, calling in jokes to my favorite radio station, buying CDs and sharing favorite songs with people, giving shoulder massages, leading a local civic club, donating my time to activities that help kids, attending church, and going to my counselor.

Question: At what point did you realize you were living the treasured life?

Mona: When a friend commented on it. She said, "I really admire the way you live. You seem so centered."

Larry: I used to be a pushover for time, money, and favors. Even if it hurt me, I'd do it anyway. Then one day an associate who had been careless with a tool I had loaned him assumed I would let him use my power sprayer. I said he couldn't and told him why. It was a very natural response. Then I knew I was living differently.

Jake: When I realized I had visited my dentist every six months for two years.

Sandy: When I ran across an old journal and saw how chaotic my life used to be.

Ann: When I designed and built my own house the very way I wanted it and filled it with things I love to do and look at.

As you can see, the treasured life is an assortment of small choices made within strong boundaries. If you were to follow any of these people through a day, you would see the signs of ownership, the evidence of boundaries, and the touches of treasuredness. You would see them letting themselves be themselves and learning what that means from moment to moment as imperfect and lovable human beings.

Like them, you are constructing your life. They would tell you, as we have throughout this book, that a better life is built on better boundaries. You are on your way to living a treasured life—one with clearly set boundaries that protect and preserve you, and present you at your finest.

References and Further Reading

Alberti, Robert, and Michael Emmons. 1982. *Your Perfect Right*. San Luis Obispo, Calif.: Impact Publishers.

Angelou, Maya. 1981. *The Heart of a Woman*. New York: Bantam Books.

Bandler-Cameron, Leslie, and Michael Lebeau. 1986. *The Emotional Hostage*. San Rafael, Calif.: FuturePace, Inc.

Berne, Eric. 1964. *Games People Play*. New York: Grove Press.

Black, Jan, and Greg Enns. 1997. *It's Not Okay Anymore, Your Personal Guide to Ending Abuse*. Oakland, Calif.: New Harbinger Publications.

Brodie, Richard. 1993. *Getting Past Okay: A Straightforward Guide to Having a Fantastic Life*. Seattle: Integral Press.

Buhler, Rich. 1991. *New Choices, New Boundaries*. Nashville: Thomas Nelson Publishers.

Burns, David. 1985. *Intimate Connections*. New York: William Morrow and Company.

Canning, Jerry. 1997. *100 Things That Don't Work and What to Do Instead.* Manuscript.

Carkhuff, Robert. 1969. *Helping and Human Relations: A Primer for Lay and Professional Helpers, Volume II, Practice and Research.* New York: Holt, Rinehart and Winston.

Carter, Jay. 1989. *Nasty People.* Chicago: Contemporary Books.

Clinebell, Howard. 1992. *Wellbeing.* San Francisco: HarperSanFrancisco.

Cloud, Henry, and John Townsend. 1992. *Boundaries.* Grand Rapids, Mich.: Zondervan Publishing House.

Csikszentmihalyi, Mihaly. 1990. *Flow: The Psychology of Optimal Experience.* New York: HarperPerennial.

Cudney, Milton, and Robert Hardy. 1991. *Self-Defeating Behaviors: Free Yourself from the Habits, Compulsions, Feelings, and Attitudes That Hold You Back.* San Francisco: HarperSanFrancisco.

Daniels, Victor, and Laurence Horowitz. 1976. *Being and Caring.* Palo Alto, Calif.: Mayfield Publishing Company.

Day, Laura. 1996. *Practical Intuition: How to Harness the Power of Your Instinct to Make It Work for You.* New York: Villard.

Efron-Potter, Ronald, and Patricia Potter-Efron. 1989. *Letting Go of Shame: Understanding How Shame Affects Your Life.* Center City, Minn.: Hazelden.

Eyler, David, and Andrea Baridon. 1991. *More Than Friends, Less Than Lovers: Managing Sexual Attraction in the Workplace.* Los Angeles: Jeremy P. Tarcher.

Firestone, Robert, and Joyce Catlett. 1981. *The Truth.* New York: Everest House Publishers.

Fossum, Merle, and Marilyn Mason. 1986. *Facing Shame: Families in Recovery.* New York: W.W. Norton and Company.

Gandy, Debrena Jackson. 1997. *Sacred Pampering Principles: An African-American Woman's Guide to Self-Care and Inner Renewal.* New York: William Morrow and Company.

Glass, Lillian. 1995. *Toxic People.* New York: St. Martin's Griffin.

Goleman, Daniel. 1985. *Vital Lies, Simple Truths: The Psychology of Self-Deception.* New York: Simon and Schuster.

Gordon, Lori, and Jon Frandsen. 1993. *Passage to Intimacy*. New York: Simon and Schuster.

Hoffman, Susanna. 1987. *Men Who Are Good for You and Men Who Are Bad: Learning to Tell the Difference*. Berkeley, Calif.: Ten Speed Press.

Horn, Sam. 1996. *Tongue Fu!* New York: St. Martin's Griffin.

Horn, Sam. 1997. *Concrete Confidence*. New York: St. Martin's Press.

Ivey, Allen. 1986. *Developmental Therapy*. San Francisco: Jossey-Bass Publishers.

James, John, and Muriel James. 1991. *Passion for Life: Psychology and the Human Spirit*. New York: Dutton.

Johnson, Marilyn. 1997. "Face to Face with Oprah Winfrey." *Life Magazine*, September, 44.

Kegan, Robert. 1982. *The Evolving Self: Problems and Process in Human Development*. Cambridge, Mass.: Harvard University Press.

Kiersey, David, and Marilyn Bates. 1978. *Please Understand Me*. Del Mar, Calif.: Prometheus Nemesis Book Company.

Klein, Marty. 1988. *Your Sexual Secrets: When to Keep Them, When and How to Tell*. New York: Dutton.

Kramer, Jeannette. 1985. *Family Interfaces: Transgenerational Patterns*. New York: Brunner/Mazel.

Kroeger, Otto, and Janet Thuesen. 1988. *Type Talk*. New York: Delacorte Press.

Kushner, Harold. 1996. *How Good Do We Have To Be?* New York: Little, Brown and Company.

Lazarus, Arnold. 1977. *In the Mind's Eye*. New York: Guilford Press.

Lerner, Rokelle. 1995. *Living in the Comfort Zone: The Gift of Boundaries in Relationships*. Deerfield Beach, Fla.: Health Communications.

Lewis, Hunter. 1990. *A Question of Values*. San Francisco: HarperSanFrancisco.

Mac Kenzie, Robert. 1993. *Setting Limits: How to Raise Responsible, Independent Children by Providing Reasonable Boundaries*. Rocklin, Calif.: Prima Publishing.

Manning, Brennan. 1990. *The Ragamuffin Gospel*. Sisters, Ore.: Multnomah Books.

Masterson, James. 1985. *The Real Self: A Developmental, Self, and Object Relations Approach*. New York: Brunner/Mazel.

Matsakis, Aphrodite. 1992. *I Can't Get Over It: A Handbook for Trauma Survivors*. Oakland, Calif.: New Harbinger Publications.

McMullin, Rian. 1986. *Handbook of Cognitive Therapy Techniques*. New York: W.W. Norton and Company.

Miller, William, and Stephen Rollnick. 1991. *Motivational Interviewing: Preparing People to Change Addictive Behavior*. New York: The Guilford Press.

Nagy-Boszormenyi, Ivan, and Geraldine Spark. 1973. *Invisible Loyalties: Reciprocity in Intergenerational Family Therapy*. New York: Brunner/Mazel.

Peck, M. Scott. 1978. *The Road Less Traveled*. New York: Simon and Schuster.

Peterson, Marilyn. 1992. *At Personal Risk: Boundary Violations in Professional-Client Relationships*. New York: W.W. Norton and Company.

Prochaska, James, John Norcross, and Carlo DiClemente. 1994. *Changing for Good*. New York: William Morrow and Company.

Rutter, Peter. 1986. *Sex in the Forbidden Zone*. Los Angeles: Jeremy P. Tarcher.

Samenow, Stanton. 1984. *Inside the Criminal Mind*. New York: Time Books.

Schneider, Jennifer, and Burt Schneider. 1991. *Sex, Lies, and Forgiveness*. New York: HarperCollins.

Snyder, C.R., Raymond Higgins, and Rita Stucky. 1983. *Excuses: Masquerades in Search of Grace*. New York: John Wiley and Sons.

Swann Jr., William. 1996. *Self-Traps: The Elusive Quest for Higher Self-Esteem*. New York: W.H. Freeman and Company.

Tye, Joe. 1997. *Personal Best*. New York: John Wiley and Sons.

Waldinger, Robert. 1990. *Psychiatry for Medical Students*. Washington, DC: American Psychiatric Press.

Yochelson, Samuel, and Stanton Samenow. 1976. *The Criminal Personality*. New York: Aronson.

Some Other
New Harbinger Titles

The End of-life Handbook, Item 5112 $15.95

The Mindfulness and Acceptance Workbook for Anxiety, Item 4993 $21.95

A Cancer Patient's Guide to Overcoming Depression and Anxiety, Item 5044 $19.95

Handbook of Clinical Psychopharmacology for Therapists, 5th edition, Item 5358 $55.95

Disarming the Narcissist, Item 5198 $14.95

The ABCs of Human Behavior, Item 5389 $49.95

Rage, Item 4627 $14.95

10 Simple Solutions to Chronic Pain, Item 4825 $12.95

The Estrogen-Depression Connection, Item 4832 $16.95

Helping Your Socially Vulnerable Child, Item 4580 $15.95

Life Planning for Adults with Developmental Disabilities, Item 4511 $19.95

Overcoming Fear of Heights, Item 4566 $14.95

Acceptance & Commitment Therapy for the Treatment of Post-Traumatic Stress Disorder & Trauma-Related Problems, Item 4726 $58.95

But I Didn't Mean That!, Item 4887 $14.95

Calming Your Anxious Mind, 2nd edition, Item 4870 $14.95

10 Simple Solutions for Building Self-Esteem, Item 4955 $12.95

The Dialectical Behavior Therapy Skills Workbook, Item 5136 $21.95

The Family Intervention Guide to Mental Illness, Item 5068 $17.95

Finding Life Beyond Trauma, Item 4979 $19.95

Five Good Minutes at Work, Item 4900 $14.95

It's So Hard to Love You, Item 4962 $14.95

Energy Tapping for Trauma, Item 5013 $17.95

Thoughts & Feelings, 3rd edition, Item 5105 $19.95

Transforming Depression, Item 4917 $12.95

Helping A Child with Nonverbal Learning Disorder, 2nd edition, Item 5266 $15.95

Leave Your Mind Behind, Item 5341 $14.95

Learning ACT, Item 4986 $44.95

ACT for Depression, Item 5099 $42.95

Integrative Treatment for Adult ADHD, Item 5211 $49.95

Freeing the Angry Mind, Item 4380 $14.95

Call **toll free, 1-800-748-6273,** or log on to our online bookstore at **www.newharbinger.com** to order. Have your Visa or Mastercard number ready. Or send a check for the titles you want to New Harbinger Publications, Inc., 5674 Shattuck Ave., Oakland, CA 94609. Include $4.50 for the first book and 75¢ for each additional book, to cover shipping and handling. (California residents please include appropriate sales tax.) Allow two to five weeks for delivery.

Prices subject to change without notice.